FIRESIDE

Enjoy it Verle —
"the best is yet
to come".
Dolores

Coping With Your Husband's

RETIREMENT

ROSLYN FRIEDMAN
AND
ANNETTE NUSSBAUM

A FIRESIDE BOOK
PUBLISHED BY
SIMON & SCHUSTER, INC.
NEW YORK

FOR MIKE AND BOB

Designed by Bonni Leon

Manufactured in the United States of America

1   3   5   7   9   10   8   6   4   2

Library of Congress Cataloging in Publication Data

Friedman, Roslyn.
Coping with your husband's retirement.

"A Fireside book."
1. Retirement—United States.   2. Husbands—United
States—Retirement.   3. Wives—United States—Effect
of husband's retirement on.   I. Nussbaum, Annette.
II. Title.
HQ1062.F67 1985   646.7'9   85-25421
ISBN: 0-671-54719-4

ACKNOWLEDGMENTS

WE FIRST CONCEIVED OF THE IDEA FOR THIS BOOK AFTER the husbands of two of our friends retired. We were witness to the very delicate adjustments they both had to make and we became aware that each of the couples had some difficult times at the beginning of retirement.

We thought of retirement as having so much promise. Wasn't there going to be the proverbial gold watch, the laudatory dinner and a life of leisure for him? But what, we wondered, was there for her? We decided to find out.

We interviewed seventy-five women, all wives of retirees. We went to their homes, met them for lunch, had them to our homes, talked to them by phone. We want now to thank them for their honesty and their confidence. We were impressed by their inner strength, their warmth and their humor. To them, we will always be grateful.

In addition, we want to give our special thanks to these professionals who helped us enormously: Nancy Ackerman, Marriage, Family and Child Counselor; Dr. Christine Friedman of the University of Southern

Maine; Dr. Jerome Grunes of Northwestern University Medical School Department of Psychiatry and Behavioral Sciences; Philip Mullenbach, investment counselor; Dr. Michael Pearlman, Boston psychiatrist; Dr. Henry Seidenberg and Dr. Arnold Tobin of the Chicago Institute for Psychoanalysis; and Dr. Barbara Vaughan of Martha Washington Hospital, Chicago.

We also extend our appreciation to Jo-Ellen Vernali-Knoerl, Albert E. Peterson and the staff of the American Association of Retired Persons in Washington, D.C. Our thanks as well to the staff of the Winnetka Senior Center, Winnetka, Illinois.

Once again, to the real experts, the wives, our sincere appreciation.

CONTENTS

1
THE RETIREMENT YEARS

FANTASY VERSUS REALITY

On the very first day of my husband's retirement, he walked into my kitchen, opened a cabinet and said, "What do you need with seven cans of anchovies?"
Millicent Landry

When you married all those years ago, you were convinced that you and your husband would live happily ever after.

Now it's the ever after. He's about to retire and if you're like many of the women you are soon to meet in this book, you're apprehensive. Will he be home all day? Will you have to keep him amused? Will you have to give up your friends? Your volunteer job? Your part-time job? Worse still, will you have to make lunch?

Make lunch! You haven't been home at noon since your youngest stayed in school for a full day. And if you have to make your husband's lunch now that he's going to be home, you can bet he won't be satisfied with peanut butter and jelly sandwiches. Somehow, being responsible for your husband's midday meal symbolizes a whole range of postretirement problems and adjustments.

We aren't suggesting that problems are inevitable, but when we turned to the experts—the seventy-five wives of retirees we interviewed for this book—we found that all but a few regarded the first year or two of their husbands' retirements as real tests of their commitment to each other. Despite the rocky times some of them experienced, not one of our interviewees mentioned divorce—a few mentioned murder, but none talked about divorce.

MEET THE EXPERTS

The wives of retirees we talked with, *and listened to*, came from low, moderate and upper income brackets. They were from varied social, ethnic and geographic backgrounds. They ranged in age from 44 to 80. Some of their husbands had planned for retirement over a period of years; some of their husbands were forced to terminate a lifetime career with but a few days' notice. Each of the women we interviewed found that her husband's retirement not only made a major change in his life, it made a major change in hers.

IT'S NOT AN END, IT'S A BEGINNING

You and your husband should be looking forward to retirement with a spirit of anticipation. It can be a period of achievement, activity and, best of all, fun. According to the magazine *Retirement Living*, if your husband retires at 65, he can expect to live until he's 81 (you'll be around until you're 84). Those are a lot of quality years to fill. Actually, both of you, if you follow a sensible health regimen, can do even better than that. You probably know already that life expectancy statistics show that the longer you live, the longer you *will* live. Actuarial tables indicate that the odds of you and your husband reaching a ripe old age together increase with each passing year. According to a report of the United States Senate Special Committee on Aging, less than 5 percent of the population was 75 or older in 1982; by 2030, almost 10 percent of the population is projected to be in that age group. By 2050, 12 percent of the entire population is expected to be 75 years or older. By the year 2030, it is likely that 21 percent of all Americans will be 65 or older, which will represent a 64 percent increase in a twenty-year span. If your husband retires before the age of 65, and you'll meet a number of women in this book whose husbands did retire early, you and your husband could possibly spend as many years together in retirement as you did while he pursued his career—perhaps more!

The point is that you and your husband have a life to fill and together you're going to have to develop a strategy to make that life worthwhile. If all works out the way it should, the two of you will be doing those things you've always wanted to do, and better yet, you'll be surprised to find yourselves doing some things you never dreamed you'd do.

THEN WHAT'S THE PROBLEM?

Planning. Not only do plans have to be made for your financial future, they have to be made for the future of your marriage. Many couples have only one definite plan upon retirement: to take a major trip. According to Albert E. Peterson, public affairs coordinator for the American Association of Retired Persons, most people plan more for a two-week vacation than they do for the rest of their lives. You and your husband are going to be together a great deal from now on—in fact, more than you ever have before. What are your plans for living? Are you going to be with each other twenty-four hours a day? Are you going to move? Are you going to travel? In our interviews we were amazed at how little communication there was between spouses about their dreams and aspirations for the future. Although they may not have discussed it with their husbands, most of the wives did have a vision of what they thought retirement life would be.

HER EXPECTATIONS

When Ellen Goodspeed, a professional writer, thought about her husband's forthcoming retirement, she had the whole scenario worked out. They would do more traveling. John had said he wanted to write about his World War II experiences in the navy, so he had a ready-made project to pursue. Since he's an avid follower of current events as well as a history buff, he would do a lot of reading and would certainly attend the excellent current events group at the local senior center. Here's the picture Ellen projected as their ideal retirement day.

7:30   *She and John rise, do their knee bends and stretches and get ready for the day.*

8:00   *They breakfast together in their kitchen, which John has just re-painted a sunny yellow.*

8:30   *She puts in a load of wash while John does the breakfast dishes.*

9:00   *She is at work in her study on her new romance novel. John fixes the kitchen faucet, weeds the flower bed and works on his book.*

1:00   *John goes to the current events group meeting. She meets a friend for a late lunch and then grocery shops.*

5:00   *This is where Ellen's fantasy gets positively romantic. She prepares a few little snacks while he gets the ice and mixes the drinks. Against a background of soft music they sit down and share their day.*

A simple fantasy. Nothing dramatic, nothing unreasonable.

The reality: John never read her scenario. After years of getting up at 6:30 a.m. to make the 7:35 train into the city, John now enjoys staying in bed and watching the morning news until 9 a.m. At 9:30 he comes down to breakfast in his robe and wants Ellen to have breakfast with him. Fixing the faucet and working in the garden are not on *his* day's agenda—nor is the current events class at the senior center. He is appalled at the idea of being thought a senior and thinks of members of senior centers as little old people being transported about in undersized school buses. As for the book he says he's going to write—well, he has to feel the inspiration to get started. Unlike his wife, who is a professional writer and is at the typewriter from three to four hours every day, John is waiting for the muse to fly in the window. As for the last item in Ellen's scenario, they do have cocktails together in the late afternoon, but it's not the intimate ritual she'd pictured. It's obvious that Ellen's fantasy collided with the reality of John's retirement.

HIS EXPECTATIONS

Millicent Landry's husband, Bruce, loves the sun and loves golf. The Landrys had vacationed in Scottsdale,

Arizona, and Bruce was counting the days until they could move to Arizona and live right on a golf course. Millicent wasn't sure, but she didn't want to put a damper on his dream. They now live in a planned retirement community in Arizona and Bruce is in heaven. He's taken about eight strokes off his golf score, plays bridge at the club two or three times a week, has become a gourmet chef and has reorganized the kitchen. And although he criticized Millicent for having seven cans of anchovies in the cabinet, he saw nothing unusual in his purchase of five bottles of capers. Bruce loves the life. Millicent hates it. She doesn't like the beastly hot weather in Arizona in the summer. She doesn't play tennis and she's not a golfer. She's put off by the fact that everyone in their housing development is approximately the same age and of the same background. She can't seem to find her niche.

Millicent has to accept some responsibility for her situation. She never really expressed her needs. If she had, it is possible that she and Bruce could have found a place to retire which would have pleased them both. But when he retired, they were focused on their investments, their pension fund, their Social Security benefits. They didn't ask, what do we *want* in retirement? All they asked was, what will we be able to *afford* in retirement?

Is Bruce a bad guy? Not really. He had a dream and he expressed his needs, but there was a breakdown in communication because Millicent was fearful of expressing her needs. She tried to live up to *his* expectations.

Is she a victim? Only of her own reluctance. She didn't speak up and her husband couldn't read her mind. But even when communication *does* take place, retirement fantasies don't always work out. Meet the Taylors.

THEY HAD A DREAM

Moving to Mexico was Kathy and Ron Taylor's fantasy after Ron retired. They had read about a little Mexican community in a travel magazine and it sounded like paradise. It was an artists' colony and the town also had a school where they could study language and take other courses. So the Taylors packed up and moved to Mexico.

It was more than they hoped for. The countryside was calm and beautiful, their U.S. dollars were valuable and they established an instant rapport with the people they met.

Living in Mexico was ideal—for five months. That's the length of time the Taylors' love affair with the new life lasted. Ron found he just couldn't let go. "He was loaded with guilt," says Kathy. "He had always been duty-bound and he had an uneasy feeling that he was doing something wicked by not doing something productive. I think one of the great things about our marriage is that I indulge in fantasies that appeal to him —that I dare to imagine doing the unexpected, while Ron has always accepted the responsibility for the sane things in our life.

"When I look back now, I realize that the whole time we were away we were getting ready to come back. Ron felt he had to be 'doing something,' and I can see that we were never really in our own territory. We were aliens in a foreign land. So after five months we packed our bags and headed for home."

The Taylors still indulge in fantasies about their future. They're young—in their early fifties—and in good health and they feel they have a lot of living ahead of them. "I've given up dreaming that everything would be better, more exciting, if only we lived somewhere else," says Kathy. "But I haven't given up making plans for the future."

The reality of retirement

Your husband might be willing to share your fantasies and expectations with you. He might even be willing to share *his* dreams with *you*, but if he's like many men, he'll be less willing to share his fears. It's imperative that you realize that his life has undergone a dramatic change and that he might be experiencing a degree of anxiety as a result of retirement.

You've been married to him for a long time; you know the signals.

According to Dr. Arnold Tobin of the Chicago Institute for Psychoanalysis, when a man does not retire by choice—if he is asked to leave his job because of age, because the job no longer exists or for any number of reasons other than his own option—he is often filled with feelings of shame, inadequacy and anger. Even if he does retire by choice, he might suffer from survivor guilt. He is not sure he deserves the luxury of not working any more and he is subconsciously afraid of other people's envy. In spite of the increasing number of retired men and the increasing number of younger and middle-aged men retiring, our culture does not help a man prepare for retirement. His feelings of shame can be translated into feelings of being unlovable. Because he is unable to cope with the changes in his life, a husband in his new role as retiree can either inadvertently or deliberately make his wife feel inadequate.

Dr. Tobin points out that a woman traditionally spends her lifetime managing other people's tensions— her husband's, her children's, her parents'. At the same time she's expected to manage her own tensions.

We women have been programmed to feel it's our responsibility to keep our husbands healthy, happy, busy and amused. After all, aren't we the ones responsible for domestic tranquillity? Thus it's not surprising that many of the women we interviewed confessed to feelings of personal guilt when their husbands were unable to make a smooth transition to retirement life.

Both you and your husband might be feeling a degree of guilt and anger, and you might not allow yourselves to identify these feelings. Many of us avoid confrontation. Consequently the hostility between a husband and wife can surface in some strange and indirect ways. For example:

Marianne Robinson's husband, Wes, was a successful engineer in a top executive position in a large corporation. When his company made staff cutbacks for economic reasons, he was forced to take early retirement. He received a generous pension so the Robinson finances were not a problem. Marianne was delighted at first. She thought this would be their opportunity to travel and to do things together that they never had the time to do before. But Wes wasn't ready. No matter what she planned, he balked. He didn't want to travel. He didn't want to go out for dinner. He didn't want to leave the house. Although Marianne realized he was depressed, she began to feel less respect for him. She had been proud of him when he was an executive; now she saw him as lazy and uncooperative. She resumed her own life, pursuing her interests and seeing her friends, and she created menial tasks for him to do around the house "just to keep him busy." One of his duties was to vacuum the carpets once a week. Unfortunately, whenever he vacuumed he gouged the walls and chipped the furniture. According to Dr. Tobin, Wes Robinson was taking out his anger with destruction by vacuum cleaner because he did not have the capacity to face his real feelings since retirement.

Of course, some postretirement problems can be more serious. In some cases a man's feelings of shame and anger are so deep that they can result in depression and even impotence.

What's a woman to do?

Communicate! Negotiate!

You've heard them often, those two key words: communication and negotiation. Unfortunately they've become buzzwords, words devoid of meaning. Do you want your husband to trade in your old station wagon for a new red convertible? You must communicate. Does your husband want to trade in the old station wagon for a black four-door sedan? He must negotiate. Now we don't mean to put down the processes of communication and negotiation, but it's all too easy to tell a woman that all she has to do for a perfect marital relationship is to communicate with her husband. Not all of us communicate that easily. Communication is supposed to be mutual, not a monologue. We can't force our husbands to become fountains of information. Most men aren't in the habit of expressing their feelings. And then there's the matter of timing. When you feel like talking, he doesn't. And when he feels like talking, you've just spilled two pounds of granulated sugar on the kitchen floor and your teeth are locked together in a permanent crunch.

You probably have an advantage over your husband when it comes to communicating your feelings. Think of your women friends in whom you confide. Most of us will talk at very personal levels to women who are mere acquaintances. In fact, we're quite open about expressing our concerns about family matters. But men rarely share personal confidences.

Dr. Michael Pearlman, a Boston psychiatrist in private practice, says that men do some very interesting commmunicating, but in a far different way than women do. Put a group of men who are casual acquaintances together and they quickly size each other up through verbal cues. Behind men's conversations about sports and business are the issues of strength and power. While they might speak to each other about personal matters in private, social conversations are impersonal. Unlike women, who can discuss intimate matters without feeling threatened, men are more guarded. Dr. Pearlman describes this response as typical of the "masculine protest," an unwillingness on the part of men to be acted upon, to be passive or to be seen as weak and out of control.

Understand that your husband might be one of those who is unable to express his wants and needs as easily as you do. The truth is that you've been married to him a long time and you should be capable of reading every cue he sends you. What we hope to do in this book is to help you establish new lines of communication with your husband now that he's retired.

We're going to stress the need to think before you speak, to know in advance what it is you want to accomplish.

We intend to demonstrate the necessity for complete honesty. Are you expressing what you really mean, or are you being manipulative?

We hope to prove the importance of mutual respect. Respect your husband's point of view and assume that he will respect yours.

Instead of simply telling you to communicate and negotiate, we will show you how the women in this book have accomplished these feats, and we will illustrate ways in which you and your husband can communicate and negotiate successfully.

*P*LAN AHEAD

If there was one salient point made by most of the wives we interviewed, it was that they wished they and their husbands had started planning for their retirement years much earlier than they did.

"Most of us worried about career choices in high school, and at the latest in the first year or two of college," said one wife we interviewed, "but we didn't think of our retirement—what we were going to do with our remaining years together—until it was upon us."

One of the experts we spoke to pointed out an interesting irony. People who face divorce have to plan their lives apart: Who will take custody of the children? What will be done with the house? What will the financial arrangements be? Divorce *forces* them to deal with questions of their future relationships. A happily married, about-to-be retired couple rarely invest nearly as much time in their future plans.

If you've been worrying about your financial future, if you've been thinking about how much time you and your husband will spend together when he retires, if you've been fretting about how much time you're going to spend apart, if you are toying with the idea of making a move to the Sun Belt or to a city apartment, if you would like to travel, if you want to get a part-time job—now is the time to start planning. It is our hope that this book will help you make some of these very important decisions.

Take the advice of one woman whose husband has been retired for five years: Set the pattern of your daily life at the very beginning of his retirement. If you make his lunch every day for the first year, it will be all but impossible to get him to make his own lunch the second year. Oh, it can be done; in fact, if you find yourself in that situation now, we're going to help you change it. In the following pages you are going to meet several women whose husbands actually became gourmet cooks.

Your future years with your retired husband should be fulfilling and fun. Marriages are dynamic, we're happy to say. Your relationship with your husband will change. That's what keeps life interesting. It also makes all things possible. If you and your husband take the time to plan your future and to be honest with each other while keeping your sense of humor, your husband's retirement years hold great promise for both of you.

*Y*OU ARE NOT ALONE

The women we interviewed for this book, all wives of men who retired or were about to retire, were most forthcoming. They allowed us to share their aspirations, their disappointments, their joys. All the women were more than happy to talk to us. In fact, they were anxious to share their personal experiences, for it was evident that many of the women we talked to felt isolated. They were convinced that their problems were unique.

It wasn't unusual for an interviewee to be amazed when told that another woman reacted to a situation just as she had. "You mean I'm not the only one?" she would reply. "I've been so angry and so guilty about feeling this way."

Don't be surprised if some of the stories the women in this book share sound like pages out of your own book.

A special note: All of the women in this book are real. All of their stories are true. Only the names are fictitious.

2
DOING
THINGS
SEPARATELY
THE NEED TO BE APART

> TED: They sent in the marines!
>
> LAURA: I have to take the clothes out of the dryer.
>
> TED: You never want to talk to me. I'm always in your way.
>
> LAURA: If I don't take them out of the dryer right away, I'll have to iron them.

Ted Pierce retired six months ago. Laura, his wife, says she loves him, says he's so much more relaxed now, says that they do so many things together. Laura also says she is suffocating. "I care about him, I really do, but we are together twenty-four hours a day. Sometimes I feel as if I just can't breathe."

Joanne Nyquist, whose retired husband, Kevin, has a tendency to shadow her footsteps as she goes about her household tasks, says that the constant togetherness of retirement makes her feel as if she were drowning. Grace Stern, whose husband, Harry, retired nine years ago, says there are days when she still feels smothered.

Unfortunately, retirement begins to sound like a female respiratory disease, and too much togetherness seems to be the virus.

No doubt you are looking forward to retirement as an opportunity to be with your husband in a way you never were before.

He will be your friend.

He will be your playmate.

He will be your lover.

He will be your full-time companion.

But wait a minute! Can you see yourself being with *anyone* twenty-four hours a day? Even the best marriage would show signs of strain from that amount of togetherness.

According to Dr. Arnold Tobin, a man faces an abrupt change in his life when he retires. Since men are defined by what they do, most of them are not prepared for the emptiness, the loss of identity that results when their careers are over. Few men seek new friendships with other men after retirement, and the relationships they do have with their men friends are less giving than those we have with our women friends; they have no one to share their crises with. They have no one to unload their frustrations on but their wives, who promised to be available for better or for worse.

We women deal with our own retirement syndromes earlier in life than our husbands do, according to Dr. Tobin. We anticipate the major emotional and physical changes in our lives. We know about the empty-nest syndrome and are not surprised at feeling a bit lost and depressed when the children leave home. We are prepared for the inevitability of menopause and most of us weather it quite well. In our rougher moments we often turn to our friends for support, and we are far less reluctant than our husbands to seek professional help if we need it.

The irony is that just when we have gotten used to the freedom of not having young children to care for, just when we have solved the problem of what to do with the rest of our lives, our retired husbands look to us to fill their empty days. They ask us to do something few of us really want to do again—to be nurturers.

Chances are your husband has never dealt with the question "What am I going to do today?" Now that he is retiring, he will not only ask that question, he will look to you to answer it. What *are* you going to do? Are you going to drop everything, quit your job, cancel your lunch date with friends and give him your undivided attention (not to mention your not-so-repressed rage)? Or are you going to kiss him good-bye, trying not to notice the abandoned look on his face, and go off to lunch carrying your smart new shoulder-strap bag filled with one thousand pounds of guilt?

THE GREAT ESCAPE
MUST YOU BE A MARTYR?

Your husband is home and definitely at loose ends. He putters a little, looks in the refrigerator, turns on the television, turns it off, and then the phone rings. You both race to answer it, and you win. It's your closest friend.

"There's a terrific sale at the May Company," she says, "and there's a sale on running shoes at Jason's— half-price; let's go shopping and have lunch."

You look at your husband and he's looking at you. Now what do you say to your friend?

When we asked Joanne Nyquist this question, she admitted she would turn down the invitation to go shopping. Her response was typical of many of the women interviewed. "I just don't feel free to leave Kevin," Joanne explained.

Kevin, 58 years old, retired after selling his electronics firm. Joanne stayed home with Kevin for the first year of his retirement. "He was very depressed," she says. "All he knew was business, and now that he was retired he didn't know what to do with himself. I was truly worried about him. He expected me to plan his days, and even when I did plan a nice day together, he would say, 'But what are we going to do tomorrow?'"

Because she did care, Joanne made effort after effort to interest Kevin in outside activities. If she set up a plan for the day, he was willing to go along with it. But when she suggested a project for him to pursue on his own, he balked. Like many men who face the adjustment of retirement, Kevin seemed to need an undue amount of nurturing. He was not ashamed to admit his dependence on his wife. The result? She felt trapped and guilty. "I really couldn't solve his problems because anything I suggested was just a short-term solution," says Joanne. "He had to find something worthwhile to do for himself."

And he did—the hard way. Joanne sprained her back and was unable to move, let alone cater to her husband. Kevin now became the nurturer. He was solicitous and he managed to get through the day just fine without her help. By the end of her recuperation he couldn't wait to leave the house with plans of his own. Now that Joanne's back is on the mend she realizes that she didn't do Kevin any good by supporting his dependency needs. When she wants to go out with her friends, she just kisses Kevin on the cheek and says she'll see him later. Joanne confesses that even now she has to resist taking the responsibility for his boredom which still occurs occasionally.

According to Dr. Jerome Grunes of the Northwestern University Medical School Department of Psychiatry and Behavioral Sciences, Kevin's reaction was not at all unusual. By the time a man reaches the age of retirement he begins to turn from his managerial tendencies to a need to be nurtured. Women at the same age tend to move to greater activity and often have a new sense of self that didn't have a chance to blossom in the earlier "mothering" years. Dr. Grunes warns that a woman might have to fight to maintain a life of her own when her husband retires. She should be sensitive to the changes he is experiencing, but she does not do her husband a service by being overprotective.

If you understand that your husband's need for nurturing when he retires is not unusual, you should be less intimidated by his dependence. Why not compromise? Try to be as supportive as you can when you are together, but make sure that you take the required time for yourself. Sacrificing your own pursuits, giving up social engagements with your women friends will do your husband little good; in fact, it will only promote his helplessness. What you can do is assure him that you care for him. You must understand that only he can solve his problem. If he knows that he has your love and approval, he'll eventually draw on his own resources. He does not need you to prescribe; he just needs you at his side.

DO YOU ASK FOR PERMISSION?

Laura Pierce does. Now that husband Ted has been retired for six months, he has agreed to let her take Fridays off to be with her friends. She has little guilt about Fridays. If she wants an additional day for herself, she asks Ted if its OK. "He never says no," says Laura. "But I still feel guilty."

Emily Shuman, on the other hand, leads what she terms an "independent life." Emily is an athletic woman who looks and acts much younger than her 60 years. Before his retirement her husband, Martin, turned to her and said, "I don't want you to change your schedule one bit when I retire. Just go about your business doing the same things you've always done." And that's just what Emily has done. She plays tennis three to five times a week, volunteers at the hospital, takes Italian lessons and an aerobics class. Husband Martin is content to stay home.

"Martin likes to read or he works at his desk," says Emily. Then she smiles. "Best of all, as long as he's home he answers the phone, lets repairmen in, and accepts packages." Lucky Emily! Her situation seems ideal. Of course, should Martin change the rules she would probably be in the same boat as Laura Pierce.

Most of the women interviewed were not as timid as Laura or quite as free as Emily, but almost all of them looked to their husbands for permission to take a day away.

Carol Fletcher is the exception. She gives *herself* permission to pursue her own interests. She doesn't feel a woman should change her lifestyle when her husband retires. So Carol plans her days much as she did when Art was working.

"Art is an adult," says Carol, "and I refuse to mother him by trying to find things to occupy him." Nor does Carol regard him as a stern father by asking him for permission to go out. "He's really my friend," says Carol. "We do many things together and many things apart."

Husbands aren't as fragile as we think. They have survived for years without our constant companionship. We're not suggesting that you aggressively demand time of your own. What we are suggesting is that you *recognize your need as being equal to his.* Which of these two dialogues would be more likely to take place between you and your husband?

Asking for Permission:

> YOU: Honey, do you mind if I meet my sister for lunch and the symphony tomorrow? She has an extra ticket.
>
> HE: Well, I thought *we'd* do something. But if you'd rather be with her...
>
> YOU: (guilty): Oh, I'm sorry, I didn't realize... OK, I'll call and tell her to get someone else.
>
> HE: No, go ahead. Do what you want.
>
> YOU: No, I'll stay home (angry and frustrated)
>
> or
>
> OK, I'll go (guilty, guilty, guilty).

Giving Yourself Permission:

> YOU: Honey, I have a date for lunch and the symphony with my sister tomorrow. I want you to know that I'll be gone most of the day.
>
> HE: I thought *we'd* do something.
>
> YOU: I'd love to do something with you. Why don't we plan a day together on Friday?

And then Friday will be a day you both look forward to.

SHOULD YOU USE SUBTERFUGE?

Meet Martha Warren. Slim and attractive, Martha is about thirteen years younger than her husband, Tom. They are very close and even worked together in their dry-cleaning business. Through the years Martha established a pattern of caring for her husband's every need. After they both put in a hard day at work, they would return home and Martha would cook his favorite meal, butter his bread and all but cut his meat for him. She admits she created a monster. Now in retirement, Tom is totally dependent upon Martha and he expects to be with her constantly. But Martha uses a ploy to get away.

"Thank God for TV," she says. "It has become a husband sitter for me. Tom likes the sports events, so if there's a good football game or baseball game on the tube, Tom watches it and I tell him that I'm going to do the marketing. (He does permit her to market and do some errands alone.) It is during some of those so-called marketing expeditions that Martha gets to do the things she's been dying to do by herself. "Of course, if I am gone more than two or three hours, he gets angry," says Martha. One afternoon when she was out longer than he thought she should have been, he called the police! They explained that a three-hour absence did not mean she was a missing person.

A number of the women interviewed used various ruses to escape. One midwestern suburban woman loves going to Chicago to visit museums and galleries. Her husband hates the city, and says trips there are too expensive. So she changed doctors. She now goes to a Chicago physician. When she sees him about once a month for a chronic but minor ailment, she also hits every art gallery on Superior Street.

Another woman interviewed uses her regular day at the beauty parlor to do some things on her own. Her appointments are taking longer and longer.

Devising ploys to get away can be a strain. Lying is exhausting.

Grace Stern is more up-front about her need to get out of the house. Grace took a part-time job. There's no way her husband can complain about her absence because she contributes money that allows them some luxuries.

Nancy Ackerman, a marriage and family therapist, says that a woman who takes a part-time job to escape too much togetherness doesn't solve her problem, she avoids it. Mrs. Ackerman feels that couples should talk over their retirement expectations in advance. Here are some questions you and your husband might ask each other:

- How do you feel about my making my own plans without consulting you first?
- How do you feel about my leaving on days on which you have nothing to do?
- Do you expect me to plan our days for both of us?
- How would we spend a typical retirement day?

You might be surprised by your husband's answers, just as he might be surprised by yours. Too often we don't communicate our expectations and then we're disappointed when our spouses don't know our needs. (The workbook in Chapter XI provides a ready-made set of questions which should help you and your husband communicate with each other.)

For example, to the question *How would we spend*

a typical retirement day?, your husband might say, "Well, we'll get up and have breakfast, then we'll watch the news and read the papers, and then we'll take a hike. Then we'll have lunch and then..."

"Wait a minute," you'll say, "I don't mind making breakfast and I don't mind taking a hike, but when do I do the laundry? And I'm always gone from noon to four."

Then he'll say, "I didn't realize that..."

It shouldn't be too long before the two of you work out a plan to your mutual satisfaction. If he knows your plans in advance, he can't be hurt if you want to do something on your own. You won't have to ask for permission and you need never feel guilty. There will be days that are less than perfection, but anyone married long enough to reach the retirement years together knows that.

SPACE WARS
WHO RUNS THIS HOUSE?

"When I look back now, I realize that during his first years of retirement (when I was still working) he usurped my authority for the management of the house. He has become 'general of the army,' taking over organization of household tasks, meal planning, and interior decorating," complains Karen Conners, a vivacious woman who continued in her job as a commercial artist for two years after her husband, Fred, took early retirement from the U.S. Army Corps of Engineers. "He reorganized the kitchen, wrote a step-by-step manual for the most efficient method of doing laundry, and argued with me about the way I cleaned the kitchen sink. I had assumed from the first that running the house would always come under my jurisdiction. When I was working I could laugh about it because I was out of the house; now that I'm not working I have a difficult time seeing the humor of it."

More than one wife interviewed said that their retired husbands had become critics of their housekeeping. Understanding, compromise and a sense of humor would go a long way in resolving the question of who is in charge when you both headquarter at home.

Dr. Jerome Grunes points out that in a traditional marriage, where the husband's basic responsibilities are outside the home and the wife's are home-oriented, the husband is defined by what he does; the wife is defined by where she is. Once a man retires there is often a subtle shift in roles. He becomes more interested in the home; at the same time she wants to expand her outside interests.

Take advantage of his new interest. Why not share household tasks; it can cut chore time to a minimum. If your husband has become your critic, telling you that you don't clean the stove the way *he'd* clean the stove, take a deep breath, pull off your rubber gloves and let him clean the stove.

Karen Conners had another complaint about her husband's push into her space.

Fred left the Corps four years ago with a comfortable pension and time to look around for an interesting job. The new job idea fell by the wayside. His hobbies and interests have expanded to fill up the day—and the house. He collects seashells, books and jazz albums. "Fred's collections spilled over into every corner of our small home," says Karen. "I knew I was letting irritations build—the trivia was taking over a good marriage. So I looked into my own feelings, my irritation with the trivia, and realized I was not going to change the patterns and attitudes Fred had developed. I felt the need for help in claiming and maintaining my personal space. So I managed to hold on to the smallest room in the house for my very own bailiwick. Fred concedes this room is off-limits to his various collections; it's decorated in a color scheme that pleases *me*, with furnishings that I chose.

"Then I enrolled in a course in transcendental meditation, much to the amusement of my husband and my 'intellectual' friends. 'TM is mystical nonsense,' said

Fred. 'Why pay good money for this silliness? If you
want to lose yourself in thought, why not look out the
window, or read a book about it?'

"I took from the course what worked for me. It frees
my mind. I learned to direct my thinking (or not thinking at all) and I can space out from the irritations that
were bothering me. I go to my room at least once a day
and meditate and even Fred recognizes the change it
has made in my life. Now when I find that small annoyances are creating tensions between us, Fred says
to me (only half in jest), 'Why don't you go and meditate?' "

It's a myth that you need less room after your husband retires. Your very own space becomes increas-
ingly important to your mental health. We all need a
degree of privacy. Whether you stake out the corner of
the den where you have your own desk or turn the
utility room into a sewing room does not matter, just
as long as you do have a place that is solely yours.

WHO WAS THAT ON THE PHONE?

"My women friends just don't call any more," says
Joanne Nyquist. "Kevin races me to the phone when
it rings, and wins. When they hear his voice my friends
think they are intruding. If *I* get the phone, he hovers
over me while I'm talking, and I become uncomfortable
and cut the conversation short."

Joanne Nyquist now has an extra-long cord on the
kitchen extension. When she settles down for a conversation she takes the phone into the adjacent laundry
room, shuts the door and speaks to her friend in a
whisper—she feels guilty about monopolizing the phone
for no "serious" reason.

Or take Laura Pierce's problem. When she's on the
phone Ted makes sure he's within earshot of the conversation and corrects her while she's talking. He'll
say, "No, it wasn't the ninth, it was the tenth." After
she hangs up he'll ask, "What was that all about?"

Laura answers, "Oh, nothing special." Ted finds it hard to believe Laura can spend twenty minutes on the phone talking about "nothing special." Since his retirement Ted has become more interested in her friends and would like to know what they have to say. Laura explains that she's not used to confiding in him. Ted is a worrier and a perfectionist and has paid for it with ulcers. Laura has always protected him from family problems with the children or with her parents because she is concerned about his health.

"I understand why he feels the way he does," Laura says. "He's bored and he wants to know everything. I have to learn to share with him."

Your husband may have calls of his own to make. There may be people he is waiting to hear from and understandably he'll expect you to share the use of the telephone. One obvious solution is the installation of a second line. But to judge from our interviews with wives of retirees, the telephone crisis goes deeper than availability of the line—it is a privacy crisis for you and a readjustment crisis for him.

Just think how important the phone has been to you. It was a major link to the outside world while you were raising your children, and even now the telephone is a partner in your social, family and community life. Recognize your husband's new interest in your telephone conversations as a need to be a part of the daytime life you have always had to yourself. If you share the day's gossip with him, he'll feel less isolated and will be less likely to monitor your phone conversations. Give him the same status as your friends. Make him your confidant.

Or why not do what Carol Fletcher did? She made a deal with her husband. She assured him that she would not intrude on his phone calls and he, in turn, agreed not to intrude on hers. "It's not that we have secrets from each other," says Carol. "It's just that it's impossible to have a phone conversation with your husband watching you and listening to every word you have to say."

*B*UT NOT FOR LUNCH

And so we come to the heart of the matter: Are you going to make lunch for your husband every day now that he's going to be home?

Joanne Nyquist made three meals a day for Kevin for over a year.

When Laura Pierce goes out on Tuesdays, she fixes lunch for Ted and leaves it in the refrigerator.

Emily and Martin Shuman have come to terms with eating schedules by going their separate ways. He gets up very late (noonish) and skips lunch. She is an early riser; half of her day is gone by the time he gets up. They try to get together every day around five for a martini and then have dinner together.

"It's important to work out your time commitments in the beginning," advises psychologist Nancy Acker-man. "Once your husband gets used to you making lunch, he's insulted when you stop. It's difficult to change routines. The wife wants the same amount of time with her husband as she had before the retire-ment. She may allow a few extra frills, but usually she does not want to spend the time nurturing him. She can say, 'I will accept the role of making dinner ar-rangements and social engagements for the evening, but I won't accept the role of being your mother and planning your day like I would for a four-year-old child.' Of course, unless she wants to do that."

Florence Quinn showed her husband how to make eggs and toast for breakfast, and since she's out of the house by the time he gets up, he makes his own break-fast every day—eggs and toast. The very same break-fast.

Doris Harris's husband has taken over more and more of the kitchen responsibility, almost by osmosis. They don't even decide on their dinner until 4:30 or 5 p.m. Then Alfred goes to the store, shops for what he wants and proceeds to make dinner. Sometimes Doris helps!

Doris's husband finds cooking a wonderful way to relax. "He finds dicing and slicing and chopping is tranquilizing," says Doris. "After thirty-eight years of cooking, I'm more than happy to let him be as tranquil as he wants."

If you're tired of cooking, if you do not want to be responsible for three meals a day, don't play the martyr. Talk it over with your husband and see if you can't arrive at a sharing arrangement. Here are some ways to help him take over some mealtime responsibilities.

- Insist that he go shopping with you so he can choose those foods he enjoys. If he knows they are in the house, he is more likely to fix them for himself.
- Send him to shop in the local deli or gourmet food shop. (There's been a proliferation of marvelous French-inspired gourmet food shops throughout the country. Expensive, yes, but worth it on occasion.) He'll have the makings of an excellent meal without having to do a thing.
- Invite him to *share* cooking chores with you. Let him make the salad while you barbecue the steak, or vice-versa. It's a beginning.
- Make sure there are sandwich meats and salad in the refrigerator when you can't be home for lunch. He can help himself. If he doesn't eat (there are still those husbands who refuse to find the refrigerator), he's the one who will go hungry. *It is not your fault!*
- Dine out! If you can't make one more lunch, go to interesting restaurants for your midday meal. It's less expensive than eating dinner out and can really perk up a day.
- Ask him to cook for you. If he presents you with a tuna salad sandwich, don't correct him because he didn't cut off the crust. Enjoy it. He might graduate to bacon, lettuce and tomato next time.

WHEN THE WOMEN GET TOGETHER

It's your turn to have your investment group meet at your house, or you want to have a luncheon for a friend who is moving away. How do you feel about having your women friends over while your husband is at home? Are you going to pack him off to a movie or ask him to hide in the bedroom?

Joanne avoids having friends over as much as she can. She waits for that rare day when she knows that Kevin is going to be busy. She doesn't feel comfortable entertaining while he is at home. "I worry about his feeling left out if he stays in the den watching television and yet I don't really want him spending the afternoon with us. I don't think he wants to do that either."

Emily has a bridge luncheon at her house once a month. She's casual and relaxed about her retired husband's presence. She asks him to join the women for a bite of lunch before they play cards. They enjoy his company; he's a warm and witty man. When it's card-playing time, he makes a polite exit. The truth is Martin doesn't take Emily up on her luncheon invitation very often, but he does know that he is welcome.

So invite your investment group to your home, or have your luncheon, but don't make your husband guess what you have in mind. Talk to him. Ask him to join you if you really want him, or explain that it's a private get-together and you'll tell him about it later.

WORKING IT OUT

Take heart. You may not believe it now, but most men who retire do not sit out the rest of their lives. Eventually they ease into new interests—business, hobbies, volunteer work—or they may make an amicable adjustment to not doing much of anything.

The too-much-togetherness blues are just a temporary malaise and you and your husband have the tools to work out the problem.

Remember:

- You are not alone. All of the women interviewed agreed that they needed some time apart from their husbands.
- It is normal for your husband to need extra nurturing as he adjusts to his retirement.
- Try to be sensitive to his needs.
- Assert your need to have time to yourself with consideration and courtesy.
- Stake out a spot in your home that is solely yours.
- Enjoy your husband's taking over some of the responsibility for the care and maintenance of your home.
- Delight in his culinary efforts.
- Communicate. Talk out your expectations of retirement with your husband.
- Love and support him but remember that you alone cannot solve his problems.

3
DOING THINGS TOGETHER

It's so damn likely that a woman is going to be left alone; she should appreciate her husband while she's got him!

Peggy Phelan

How many activities do you and your husband share? Are your evenings spent playing chess together? Do you both read books on military history and discuss them in depth? Do you spend many a Sunday afternoon in the kitchen together—he whipping up a soufflé while you stir your wok? Not if you're like most of the women we interviewed.

Most admitted that before their husbands' retirements their marriages were weekend affairs. "Oh, we were together every evening during the week, but after dinner Larry would collapse in front of the television set, and I folded the laundry," says June Shore. "The weekends were busy when our family was growing up, but I can't say we did an awful lot of things together. On Saturday Larry played tennis and got the car washed. I did the week's shopping; then there was the lawn to mow, storm windows to put up or down, and the grandparents came to visit us on Sunday. Our real time together was on Saturday night when we went out to a movie or had dinner with friends. But now that Larry has retired and the children are grown and gone, now it's all going to be different." Or is it?

IMPASSE

Ellen Goodspeed thought that when her husband, John, retired, every night would be Saturday night. She was sure that free of the pressure of work John would be thrilled to go to the theater during the week, would take a Tuesday night square-dance class, would be willing to be weaned from watching television reruns. He not only wasn't willing—he refused.

John uses a number of excuses when he rains on Ellen's parade. He hates trips into the city from his suburban home because he commuted for years and right now enjoys not having to hit the expressways. He objected to the square-dance class because he would feel foolish prancing about with a group of strangers. "I've given up," says Ellen. "It's just not worth the effort."

Ellen sees John as uncooperative and finds herself being resentful when *he* suggests some things they might do together. "Why should I be thrilled about going to his college reunion when he won't go to the theater with me?" Impasse.

Susan Powers isn't angry; she simply accepts the fact that she and her husband, Don, have different interests. "Don is a sports nut. I like the ballet. When the San Francisco Ballet is in town, I wouldn't dream of asking Don to go with me. I know he'd be bored to death. I take my daughter if she isn't busy, or I try to get a friend to go with me. On occasion I go alone."

Does Susan go to the football or basketball games with Don? "I don't know the first thing about basketball, and the only thing I know about the Super Bowl is that's the day I always make a huge pot of chili."

Susan shakes her head. "I did think it would be different once Don retired. About all we ever do together is what we did before—go out to dinner with friends and watch television."

Susan and Don have a good relationship. Although she does wish they did more things together, she isn't hurt or angry because he doesn't share her interests. But retirement life could be more fulfilling if she followed Laura Pierce's example.

ENDING THE IMPASSE

When Laura Pierce's husband, Ted, was active in business, Laura tailored her life to suit his. Ted was in a stressful, high-powered position, and Laura protected Ted and rarely demanded he do anything he didn't want to do. "I really love to travel," says Laura, "but Ted preferred spending vacation time at home. No European trips for him." When Laura did travel she went with her daughter or her mother.

But after Ted retired he started to show signs of boredom, and that's when Laura thought the time was ripe to have a talk with her husband that would change their retirement life. Laura has a nice, even way of expressing herself. She is able to make her needs clear without becoming defensive. "I told him that traveling without him wasn't much fun. 'Look,' I said, 'now that you're retired we can share some great times together if we each have a little give. I'll give things you like to do a try if you'll do the same for me.'" Ted couldn't refuse. He took his first trip to Europe with Laura and to his great surprise he enjoyed it. He is now in charge of travel plans for their next trip, a tour of Ireland.

ENJOY WHAT HE ENJOYS

What starts out as a favor to your husband may turn into a favor to yourself. That's what happened to Bernice Webber. Bernice, who is 67 years old, is taking swimming lessons at the local YMCA. She is learning to swim because her husband, Joe, likes to swim and he wanted her to join him when he did his thirty laps each day. Bernice was torn; she had a lifelong fear of water but admitted she didn't enjoy seeing Joe having so much fun without her. She took the plunge. The midmorning visit to the pool is now part of the Webbers' regular routine. Bernice is delighted with herself for overcoming her fear and she's never felt more fit.

Loosen up. Does your husband hug the television set on weekend afternoons during the football season? Be daring. Make some popcorn, get some cold drinks and sit down next to him. If you want to be a real heroine ask him to get tickets for the two of you for the next home game. After he recovers from the shock, your husband may be so appreciative of your effort to share one of his enthusiasms that he'll agree to share some of yours.

Della and Harry Nagle are best friends. There is real love and affection between them. He likes her sense of humor; she thinks he's close to genius at fixing things, and tells him so. She talks a lot; he is quiet. Della and Harry are nourishers—they are very supportive of each other.

Retirement for Harry, an oral surgeon, came at the age of 54 and it was a real shock to both of them. Harry has a degenerative eye disease and is partially sighted. After the diagnosis was made he realized he could not risk continuing his dental practice. "It was very hard to adjust at first," said Della. "We moved from a large home to a city apartment, but we made the adjustment and we're busy every minute." The Nagles walk almost every day—hike is a better word. When asked if they do their walking in the morning, Della laughed. "The great thing about retirement is that you can do things when you please. We take a walk when we feel like it—sometimes in the morning and sometimes in the afternoon."

Because Harry's eyes are affected and reading and

going to the theater are difficult, music has become one of his consuming interests. The Nagles attend concerts, belong to a baroque music society and are board members of a symphony organization. It is clear that Della has become genuinely fond of music but she admits it is important because it is something they can enjoy together.

"We do what we want to do. If I turn down a date to be with my women friends, it's because I want to," asserts Della. "Harry encourages me to go to luncheons but I just don't care for luncheons and bridge games. Don't misunderstand. I like my women friends and I do see them, but I'd rather be with Harry."

HE DOES WHAT SHE WANTS

George Gordon is a naive painter—an artist who is unschooled and untrained. George is represented by a top art dealer in Chicago, all because his wife, Cecile, insisted that he join a painting class offered once a week in their condominium recreation room. George wasn't always a painter; he was a butcher before he retired. Cecile, who designs and makes quilts, said, "I knew that my husband, who is an active person, had to do something with his time or he would be very unhappy. I hoped that dabbling with paints would be a pleasant way for him to spend a few hours each week while I worked on my quilts." Cecile and George are candid with each other, and he was willing to act upon her suggestion because he didn't feel manipulated. The Gordons, who often took three-day trips to arts and crafts fairs, discovered a group of artisans who display their handiwork in shopping malls in small towns throughout Illinois. The artists exhibit their work under the auspices of an umbrella organization called the Greying Generation.

Started in 1978 with four or five artisans, the Greying Generation now has a mailing list of 1,700 in the Chicago area who receive a newsletter three times a year; many of those on the list participate in some of the thirty-five to forty shows held each year. "The philosophy behind the Greying Generation," says Ted Kessler, a leather worker and founder of the organization, "is to give retired people something to do, a chance to be recognized for their creativity, to make a little extra money, and to meet new people." The only qualifications to become a member are that the artist must personally create the items displayed for sale, must be 55 or older and must accept responsibility for keeping the display space neat.

"We loved being part of the arts and crafts group," says Cecile. "We would pack a picnic lunch, set up our stall, display my quilts and his paintings with the other artisans, and meet interesting and friendly people who came to look and buy at the weekend arts and crafts fair. It's like an extended family—people really want to help each other. One craftsman, whose specialty was creating model airplanes from beer cans, was literally swamped with empties when he casually mentioned he was running out of supplies."

It was at one of these fairs that everything changed for the Gordons. A well-known Chicago art dealer admired George's paintings and it was then that George learned he was a "naive" painter. George paints scenes from his imagination. Born and brought up in the city, he paints pictures which tend to include silos and barns, pigs and cows. The dealer arranged for George to enter a painting in an art competition sponsored by McDonald's. George won third prize. His work is now being shown in a Chicago art gallery.

"George, who could never sit still for more than two minutes before, now sits for hours working at his easel," says Cecile. "He is proud of the surprising recognition he is receiving, and if I criticize something about a painting, he'll say, 'What do you know about it?'"

George still goes with Cecile to the art fairs and helps her set up her booth. "The only hitch," says Cecile, "is that George can't exhibit his paintings at the arts and crafts shows any more. His dealer has exclusive rights to his work." Ah, well—the price of success!

*T*AKE THE INITIATIVE

Remember, you've been a self-starter for years. Taking the responsibility for filling your own time has been an intrinsic part of your life. But it's all new to your husband.

Many of the wives interviewed expressed the fear that their husbands would sit down in front of the television set one day and never get up. Martha Warren was convinced that that was what happened to her husband, Tom.

Martha is an attractive, energetic, very young 66-year-old woman. She has a good figure, excellent skin and great energy and vitality. Her husband, Tom, is 79. This is a second marriage and they have been married over thirty-five years. He is straight and tall and looks younger than he is. He is quite attractive—the handsome younger man is still there. The only apparent signs of his aging are a fading memory, which annoys him enormously, and a tendency toward depression from boredom. Martha never felt the age difference until his retirement. She realized that when he was in business Tom seemed young and interested and is convinced that if she keeps her husband involved and active, she will be able to stave off the aging process. Martha is ingenious at getting him out of his chair in front of the television set and out of the house.

She doesn't ask Tom what he wants to do. "We'd never do anything if I made him come up with the ideas," she says. And she doesn't ask if they should go on a picnic or drive to a new shopping mall. "I just say I've made a picnic lunch and we're going to the beach today. And he really seems happy to have plans."

The Warrens have made a hobby out of finding new restaurants, particularly those that feature early-bird specials. "We go at about four o'clock and get the most elegant meals at bargain prices," says Martha. "If you have the very same meal at 7 p.m. it costs twice as much!" Martha and Tom study the weekend entertainment guides in the Fort Lauderdale and Miami newspapers. They talk over the restaurant ads and try places that seem unusual. They don't necessarily choose restaurants that their friends recommend or that they've heard about. "We really take chances," says Martha. "But for the most part we've been pretty lucky. Some of the places we've tried have been losers, but there are several that have become real favorites of ours."

Another self-starter is Pearl Richman. Like Martha, she sees television as the enemy. Her husband, John, a lawyer—intellectual, articulate, scholarly—retired and started watching "Leave It to Beaver" reruns. Pearl got busy. She enrolled both of them in a book group and a movie group. "The movie group meets once a month, and it certainly hasn't been dull," says Pearl. "Last month the leader assigned a Fellini movie and later, at the discussion, no two people agreed on its meaning. It degenerated into a shouting match until John stepped in with an analysis that was brilliant. I was so proud of his ideas that I took a back seat and basked in his reflected glory. Of course, I didn't agree with a word he said!"

If you feel that your husband has a deeper relationship with Channel Five than he does with you, why not follow the example of Martha and Pearl. Take the initiative. It's all in the way you do it.

IT'S A MATTER OF APPROACH

You're fed up. Your days have been the same for months. Life is routine. You and your husband are in the house at the same time but you're not on the same wavelength. You'd like to do things together. Now how do you intend to do it?

The "Why Don't We Ever" Approach

To be avoided at all costs is the "Why don't we ever" approach. It goes something like this:

SHE: (This must be said with a whining voice) Why don't we ever *do* anything?

HE: Hm.

SHE: All you ever do is sit in front of the television. The Lawtons always do interesting things together, but we never do anything.

HE: Did you see that play at third base?

SHE: That's all you ever do, just sit. Why don't we take a course in raising bonsai trees like the Lawtons?

HE: Who are the Lawtons?

The "What Should We Do Today" Approach

Slightly less annoying but equally unproductive is the "What should we do today" approach.

SHE: Honey, why don't we get out today?

HE: Good idea.

SHE: What would you like to do?

HE: I don't care. Anything you want to do.

SHE: No. I asked first. What do you want to do?

HE: I don't know. You want to go to the boat show?

SHE: Oh, I don't know. It will be jammed, and we can't afford a boat. Should we go to a movie?

HE: No, we can always do that.

SHE: Why don't you ever want to do anything?

HE: Did you see that play at third base?

The "Take the Initiative" Approach

This might take a bit of courage since it might not be your usual style, but try this approach once or twice and you might be surprised at the results.

SHE: Don't make any plans for tomorrow—we've got a big day ahead of us.

HE: We do? What's happening?

SHE: We're going to drive to Milwaukee. I've been dying to see the art museum.

HE: Drive to Milwaukee?

SHE: And then we're going to the Milwaukee Zoo.

HE: The zoo?

SHE: We sure are. You know some good restaurants in Milwaukee. Why don't you pick out a good one for dinner?

HE: We've got to go to Ratzch's. I haven't been there in years.

SHE: Did you see that play at third base?

TAKE IT EASY

Now that you and your husband are going to have the luxury of leisure time, are you going to panic and push to fill every waking moment with productive activity? You might miss something if you do. Burt and Shirley Waterman are frenzied in their pursuit of togetherness. When he first aired his intention to retire, it took Shirley less than forty-eight hours to come up with a marathon game plan to which Burt agreed.

They would take a course in computer science. They would join a health club and exercise together. They would study Spanish and French and then visit Spain and France. They would master the art of Chinese cooking. They would take golf lessons. And they would learn to rumba.

The Watermans were so serious about having fun that they left no time in their breakneck schedule to just relax and enjoy themselves and each other.

Doing less but enjoying more are Jenny and Roger Hubbard. The Hubbards love baseball and gossip, in that order. They own a share of stock in a National League team and follow the club avidly. They go to spring training and even take a few road trips each year. They both enjoy watching television, particularly during the baseball season.

"Roger and I are best friends," says Jenny. "In fact, we know each other so well that there isn't any need to make conversation, and when we do talk, it's often gossip." Jenny and Roger spend a great deal of time together and she never feels smothered by her husband's presence. "I'm more dependent on him than he is on me. Of course, I do go out with friends, and he plays golf several days a week, but on the whole we are with each other and we like it that way."

Very often Jenny will invite friends for lunch and include Roger. He gets along well with her friends and enjoys the gossip. "When Roger plays golf with his buddies," says Jenny, "I expect him to report back with any interesting bits of information that he may have picked up."

But the most important activity for the Hubbards is watching baseball, and if that means sitting together in front of the television set—so be it.

If you see television as the enemy, you may have fallen into a trap. Remember, television is something that can be watched in companionable silence. The Eric Garlands are proof of that. They both play golf—but not together. They both play tennis—but not together. However, there is one thing they always do together: every day at the same hour they drop whatever they are doing and settle down in front of the television set—together—to watch "All My Children." Good for the Garlands. They are at that wonderful stage in life when they don't have to worry about what people think, and they don't have to please anyone but themselves.

CHILDREN'S CHILDREN

Emily and Martin Shuman are independent spirits. They do very little together, except when their grandchildren arrive for a visit. Then the two of them become as one. It's off to Great America, the beach, the movies or just the backyard, but it is definitely a team project. It's not unusual for the two grandparents to help their grandchildren with their studies. "We sit across from each other," says Emily, "and we each tutor. I'm the expert in language and social studies and Martin handles science and math."

Dorey and Alan Plumb did something with their grandchildren they would never do on their own. They went to Disney World for the weekend.

"It was great," says Dorey. "Our daughter and son-in-law just had their third child, a little boy, and they were so grateful when we took the two older girls on this outing. We covered every inch of Disney World and stayed at the Disney hotel." The Plumbs had a ball.

"When we returned from Florida, we took the girls home and then went directly to our house and got into bed at 4:30 in the afternoon. We were just going to take a nap, but we didn't get up until the next morning," says Dorey.

If you're lucky enough to have grandchildren, make it a joy of retirement to enjoy them—you and your husband together.

PLAYING DANGEROUS GAMES

We all thrive on a little competition at times; it makes us try to do our best. David Lewis is a championship bridge player. Now that he's retired he knows the schedule of every duplicate bridge game in the area. His wife, Deborah, plays a fairly good game herself. She's not quite the expert that David is, but she has her own collection of master's points. Do they play bridge together?

"We did for a while," says Deborah, "and it nearly led to mayhem." The Lewises found it was too difficult to play bridge as partners although they are good partners in other areas of their marriage. David has a tendency to be critical of Deborah's play, and Deborah is so defensive she doesn't play as well with David as she does with her friend Florence as a partner. "We've solved the problem," says Deborah. "We both play bridge at the local duplicate bridge club every Tuesday evening. I play with Florence and he plays with one of his male partners, then we all go out together for coffee afterwards." Deborah and David love to talk bridge, love to play bridge. They just don't play as partners.

When Marilyn and Bob Biondi play mixed doubles at their tennis club, they often switch partners. "I can't stand when Bob yells 'up! up! up!' every time he wants me to go to the net, and then immediately yells 'back! back! back! every time he wants me to go for a lob. I run myself frantic and I feel his disapproval. When we play with our best friends, the Hoppers, I play with Lew Hopper and Bob plays with Lew's wife, Iris. The men are polite. We have a good time, and then we go into dinner as friends."

You may enjoy playing bridge and tennis together as a team. On the other hand, competing as a couple against another couple can bring out the worst in each of you. If you enjoy the game so much that you're willing to overlook your anger at his mistakes and his fury at yours, we congratulate you. Or you can follow the example of the Biondis and the Hoppers and switch partners.

Less dangerous is one-on-one competition. The Richmans love backgammon. They have an ongoing competition that's lasted almost five years. "We're about equal in skills at the backgammon table. It's fun to play and we even carry a small set with us when we travel," says Pearl.

You and your husband may be gin rummy players or Scrabble players or Boggle players. If you are, you already have an enjoyable way to spend an evening or an afternoon together. Marilyn and Bob Biondi are nuts about puzzles. They used to fight over who would get the Sunday *New York Times* puzzle. "But now we've solved it," says Marilyn. "Bob does the big crossword and I do the acrostic, the diagramless, the cryptic puzzle and the ones with puns and anagrams." Marilyn smiles as she confides, "The ones I do are much more difficult."

LOVE IN THE AFTERNOON

Sex in the morning. Sex in the evening. Sex in the afternoon. What a wonderfully wicked idea.

When in your marriage were you able to be completely spontaneous about sex? Probably the only time was when you were on vacation. Daytime sex is rarely enjoyed by working husbands and busy mothers. Not so in retirement. Your sex life can improve now that you are free to be together whenever you want.

At least that's the opinion of Dr. Barbara Vaughan, a sex therapist affiliated with the Martha Washington Hospital in Chicago. She states that with the reasonably good health of both partners there is no reason why a married couple's sexual life can't improve in later years. "Women have the freedom from the worry of pregnancy, they have the advantage of a lifetime of experience to know what works and what doesn't in their sexual relationship, and they have the stimulation and adventure of entering a new and justifiably self-centered phase of life," says Dr. Vaughan.

Many of the women interviewed said that their sex lives had improved since their husbands' retirements; only a few complained that their sex lives were negatively affected. Many reactions were typical of Joanne Nyquist's when asked about her sexual relationship with her husband. She was thoughtful for a moment and then said, "We've always had a good relationship, but now that he's retired he's become more interested in sex. I have to admit that it came as a surprise to me." She didn't seem to mind.

Don't be surprised if your husband exhibits increased sexual interest after retirement. According to Dr. Jerome Grunes, this renewed interest can be an expression of his more tender qualities—something he might not have been able to express while he was fighting it out in the marketplace. Your being open to this added attention can be liberating for you as well. If you've bothered to read the multitude of articles recently published on sex and aging, you know that there are few reasons why women and men cannot be sexually active into the very late years of their lives, if they *want* to be active.

There is every indication that the more sexually active you are, the more sexually capable you'll be. And an encouraging footnote from Dr. Vaughan: "It's never too late for sexual reawakening. Even those women and men who have been without partners for long periods of time frequently are able to find sexual stimulation and satisfaction under the right set of circumstances. And if nature is unable to bring your sex life together up to your desires, you'll find that medical science has made giant strides in therapeutic rehabilitation that may be the answer for you."

It's good to remember that the largest erogenous zone of your body is your skin. Sexual intercourse isn't always necessary. Being near to each other, fondling, caressing and loving each other is a lovely way of being together.

GET GOING

Here are but a few of the things that our interviewees did when they realized that life had become too routine:

  • Martha and Tom Warren checked into a hotel in their own hometown, taking advantage of the weekend bargain rates. They had what amounted to a mini-honeymoon.

  • Carol and Art Fletcher enrolled in a real estate course which prepared them for the state board exam. They now dabble in real estate together.

  • Florence and Peter Quinn play financiers together. Florence has taken equal responsibility for the investment of their retirement funds. They talk over all decisions, watch the market reports together and have taken a financial planning course together.

• Betty and Stan Kaplan went grudgingly to a square-dance class with some friends about five years ago. They never dreamed that square dancing would become a passion for both of them. It is their major interest now and they participate with several square-dance groups in their city.

• Dolores and Sid Paulsen love the theater. Realizing they could never see all of the plays they would like to see, they organized a play-reading group that is thriving. Both found they were frustrated actors and enjoy taking part in the productions.

• Minna and Perry Strand don't have a chance to be bored. Their home away from home is the local senior center, where they create as well as participate in activities. Minna organized the Friday Sewing Bee into a crafts-for-sale project. Thanks to her initiative, clever shoppers know they can always find an unusual handmade gift, reasonably priced, at the center, which benefits from the sale. Perry is the anchorman of an ongoing chess tournament, and he also serves on the center's board of directors.

• Rosemary and Walter Smith became deeply involved in a food and clothing distribution program run by their church. They get personal satisfaction from the days they volunteer and have expanded their network of friends to include other couples involved with the project. Any volunteer job can turn into a team project.

• Glenna and Harold Stark both work in the museum of natural history. Glenna volunteered as a docent at the museum first, and then wooed her husband into volunteering two days a week in the museum's photography department. Harold, a retired doctor, is an accomplished photographer with his own darkroom at home. The museum is an interest they can share without crowding each other's space.

• Peggy Phelan and her husband, Ned, became cooks together. They took a course in Cordon Bleu cooking and take turns being chef and *sous chef* in the kitchen. They do not share doing the dishes; Ned does them. How Peggy accomplished this is too deep for us to fathom. *Note*: The cooking doesn't have to be French. One retired couple we know are experts at cooking low-fat, low-salt natural foods.

These are a few of the things couples do together. All you have to do is get going.

A REPRISE

Just a reminder on how to connect with your husband so that you both enjoy each other's company.

- Take the initiative. Make plans instead of waiting for him to make them.
- Be willing to compromise. If he tries square dancing because you like square dancing, then you try something he would like to do.
- Take a chance. Don't be afraid to risk your time. Try an activity that's totally new. What if the lecture is boring, or the art class isn't for you? At least you tried.
- Enjoy your quiet times together. If the two of you are each reading a book, side by side, in comfortable silence, what's wrong with that?
- Forget about the Joneses. Don't care if they are always on the go to their ballet classes and polo matches. You and your husband have earned the right to do just what the two of you want to do!

4
HITTING
THE
ROAD

*We found the camper's life is
not for us. Our next trip is
going to be around the world
on standby.*
Michelle Morris

It's a rare couple whose very first plans after retirement aren't for travel, and with good reason. One of the greatest gifts retirement has to offer is freedom—the freedom to travel *when* one pleases. No more battling crowds during Christmas week. No more worry about reservations a year in advance. You and your husband can take off in January, June or July. You can plan trips for the economical off-season or, better yet, take off on the spur of the moment.

We don't doubt that both of you have already done your share of traveling, but his retirement will offer you an opportunity to be more creative in planning your trips. Before it was two weeks' vacation with pay. Now you can follow your own lights. Be daring; risk adventure!

TRY SOMETHING NEW

Bernice and Joe Webber were fairly seasoned travelers. When they were high school teachers in the public school system, they planned and took a major trip each year during summer vacation. When they retired on a fairly limited income, made even more limited by inflation, they weren't sure they could afford to continue their travels. "We wondered if we would ever be able to return to some of our favorite European countries, or if we would be able to explore new places," says Bernice. "Then we found out about Elderhostel and our problems were solved. It's a no-frills way to travel and see the world."

Elderhostel is perfect for retirees on limited budgets who want to travel and reach out to new experiences. An international network of 700 cooperating colleges and universities, the Elderhostel program offers a variety of courses. Here are a few titles from an Elderhostel catalog: "The East End of London and Its People," "The Baroque Art of Rome," "Drugs, Hormones, Sex and Madness."

The Webbers aren't afraid of roughing it. "You have to be willing to live in a college dormitory. The meals, although wholesome, are definitely *not* gourmet," says Bernice. "But the lectures and programs are fascinating and there's a marvelous mix of people from other countries."

The Elderhostel study sessions are one or two weeks long. While the Webbers usually enroll in literature and political science courses, they confess that the location of the school counts more than the course offering when they choose their Elderhostel vacation. They have gone Elderhosteling in both the United States and Europe. "We travel by car in this country and keep returning to schools located in Pennsylvania because it's such a beautiful state," says Bernice. "We go back to explore Civil War battlefields, glorious mountain trails and small towns off the main highway that have kept their Early American flavor.

"We had an unforgettable three weeks in the British Isles—one week at a college in Scotland; one week in Ireland, where we studied political history; and one week at an Elderhostel in Brighton, England, where we studied English literature. Since we had received our English literature assignments in advance we came to the course reasonably prepared to discuss the work of four authors: Rudyard Kipling, Virginia Woolf, Graham Greene and Henry James. The class met for discussion in the morning. Then in the afternoon the group took off to visit sites where these authors had lived, worked and died.

"The students were from such diverse cultural backgrounds that they didn't always see things the same way. We had three psychologists in the class who kept arguing with each other. Fortunately the instructor was extremely skilled and at the end of the week we gave him a standing ovation. Then it was off to Scotland."

The Webbers are going to Scandinavia this year. They plan to spend one week in Norway, one week in Sweden and one week in Denmark. They will study the history of each country, its people and politics, in small colleges away from major metropolitan areas.

"The trick with Elderhostel is to get your application in early so you can go to the country you want and register for the seminars that appeal to you," warns Bernice.

(For information regarding Elderhostel, write: Elderhostel, 100 Boylston Street, Boston, MA 02116.)

FIND A FOCUS

Do you love theater? New York is great, but have you visited theater festivals in Stratford—Canada *or* England? The Goodman Theatre in Chicago, the Actors

Theatre in Louisville, the Alley Theatre in Houston, the Globe Theatre in San Diego, the Guthrie in Minneapolis—the list goes on—have been seminal influences in some of the most exciting theater made in America. Any one of the regional theaters will be happy to send you a brochure of its current season; many of them have a number of shows in repertory and are located in regions you might not have had occasion to visit before.

Is architecture your major interest? Visit Barcelona and see Antonio Gaudi's epic work firsthand, or try Chicago for the early work of Frank Lloyd Wright, Louis Sullivan and Ludwig Mies van der Rohe.

Is bird watching your thing? One couple we know who were visiting relatives in England took a three-day bird-watching side trip to Majorca.

Travel without a purpose can be aimless; travel with a purpose doesn't limit you, it opens up new vistas.

TAKE A TRIP TO YOUR PAST

Marilyn and Bob Biondi recently took a trip to England to visit his World War II haunts. They went to a little village outside of Norwich to find the spot where he was stationed with the Eighth Air Force. The setting was sylvan—lovely cottages surrounded by flowers dotted the landscape. The Air Force living quarters had been interspersed through the village. "I could see where the foundations of the old Quonset huts were," said Marilyn. "Bob pointed to one cracked foundation and said, 'I'm sure this is where I lived when I flew the Berlin raid over Germany.'" A man tending his garden nearby spotted the Biondis and asked them if he could be of any help. Bob explained that he had been stationed in the man's backyard when he was in the Eighth Air Force during World War II. "That's amusing," the Englishman replied. "I was in the RAF and I was shipped to America to train pilots." Marilyn, Bob and their new English friend spent a delightful afternoon in a local pub trading war stories.

Of course, the Biondis enjoyed the Tower of London and the visit to Windsor Castle, but the trip to Norwich was special.

Iris and Mel Sanderson drove to Columbus, Indiana, where she had spent her teenage years. They toured the scenes of her childhood and had a dinner reunion with high school friends she hadn't seen in forty years. High school and college reunions are wonderful excuses to travel.

Rosemary and Walt Smith schedule their travel plans to dovetail with their hobby of genealogy. Walt, the son of a missionary, was born and raised in Cuba. As a boy, he saw his relatives only when his parents took him on infrequent trips to the United States. When he was about 17, he began keeping charts of "who begats" and taking down oral histories of aunts and uncles when he had an opportunity to see them. Even at that early age he wanted to capture the sense of belonging to an extended family that he had missed in his life. Walt has continued digging for his family history during his adult life. "I've become involved in Walt's research," says Rosemary, who was a librarian before she retired, "especially those trips that have taken us to Mexico, Spain, England, France, Sweden and Portugal."

The Smiths met and married when they went to Earlham College (a church-oriented Quaker school) more than forty years ago, so it's not surprising that their interests and hobbies continue to revolve around activities of the Society of Friends. "Part of the fun is researching church records—Quakers are known for their record keeping and at one point we discovered that our Quaker ancestors stood witness at each other's weddings as far back as the early 1700s."

The Smiths belong to three genealogical clubs and will travel anywhere to attend genealogical workshops. Their trips out of the country satisfy the travel desires of both of them. His agenda includes visits to the town

hall to meet with the records clerk, then a stop at the
local graveyard. Her agenda includes sightseeing and
occasional shopping. "I'm not enthralled with the idea
of poring over ancient death records," says Rosemary,
"and I happily forgo the gravestone rubbing." Together,
the Smiths go to restaurants and museums she has
discovered on her sightseeing bus tours.

You may neither want nor be able to trace the roots
of your family tree to the ninth century, but many
retirees take journeys back in time as a vacation theme.

NOW YOU HAVE THE TIME

If you have taken a cruise, you know how sybaritic and
satisfying life at sea can be. But cruises can be expensive. Eric and Anna Lund found a way to go to sea for
far less money than most luxury cruises cost.

Eric took early retirement from his government job
after a disagreement with a new political administra-
tion. He and Anna wanted to get away—they wanted
time together to rethink their lives and rest after a
harrowing career experience. So they bought a copy of
Freighter News, found a Norwegian freighter scheduled for a two-month run to Mediterranean ports-of-
call and signed up for the round trip.

Ten passengers boarded the freighter when it de-
parted New York. Four left at the first landfall; only
one other couple remained aboard for the entire two
months.

"Our friends asked us, 'How will you be able to bear
it? Two months of absolutely nothing to do!'" says Anna.
"But it was made for us. You have to feel good about
yourself and about the person you're traveling with to
go on a slow boat to nowhere. We made no day-to-day
plans; we simply took time to become reacquainted. We
read, we exercised—early to bed for lots of rest gave
us energy for port calls. It was first-class all the way.
The food was wonderful; our clothing needs were minimal; each port of call was a new adventure. It isn't

something I would recommend to younger people who might get restless. It *is* confining. But the trip gave us exactly what we needed—time to put our lives together again.

"It was a fantastic buy. Ordinarily, a two-month trip would have eaten up a good portion of our savings. We went by freighter at a fraction of the cost."

The Lunds' first sea trip increased their taste for ocean travel at bargain prices. The next trip out was aboard a cruise ship—Eric as a guest lecturer discussing life in the diplomatic corps, Anna speaking about the life of a diplomat's wife. They were able to travel free of charge. They got their plum assignments through a friend of a friend with connections at a steamship company. Whether drawing on their own inner resources during the two months aboard the freighter or becoming social resources for other passengers aboard the cruise ship, Anna and Eric used a lot of imagination and comparatively little cash to travel the sea lanes.

Freighters are excellent bargains, costing less than one-half the fare of cruise ships and giving passengers many more weeks of travel. Some advice: On freighters you have to be willing to stay in port as long as your ship needs to be there to unload and load its cargo. And you should be in reasonably good health because medical facilities on freighters are limited.

WHY NOT DO YOUR OWN CHARTERING?

Marilyn and Bob Biondi did. Marilyn dreamed of a trip to the Greek Islands. Bob agreed—wasn't she willing to go to his old Air Force base in England? Unfortunately, most of the cruise ships seem to whisk their passengers from one island to another in record time. "We wanted a more leisurely and informal trip," says Marilyn. Since they were not Greek shipowners and had no little yacht of their own, they chartered one and found they could play jet-set at bargain prices.

It started with an ad Bob found in *The New York*

Times advertising small yachts available for charter in the Aegean, complete with crew. The Biondis invited three other couples to join in the venture. When the price of the yacht they chartered for two weeks was divided four ways, it was less than a stay at most resort hotels.

"The cost of food and liquor was really quite reasonable," says Marilyn. "We got duty-free prices on liquor. We even picked up some caviar that was amazingly cheap. The only thing we had trouble finding was popcorn. We finally located a supply and gave it to our wonderful cook on board to prepare as a snack. His only mistake was that he thought the popcorn was breakfast cereal and he served it with sugar and cream." The four couples felt like royalty.

"The cost of yacht charters has gone up since we took our first one, but so has everything else," says Marilyn. "You have to shop around. We read yachting magazines and kept an eye out for charters in the Caribbean as well as the Mediterranean. A call to the Greek Tourist Bureau can give you a lot of information, too."

A word to the wise: it helps to be a good sailor. Charter yachts are not as steady as cruise ships in rough weather. Also, if you are traveling with two or three other couples, it's a good idea to lay down the ground rules before you set out since you'll be spending a lot of time with other couples in very close quarters. Respect each other's privacy and understand that everyone doesn't have to do everything together.

DON'T BE A TRAVEL SNOB

Do you turn up your nose at tours? They are too programmed, too superficial for your tastes? You have a point, but keep an open mind. Some tours can be blessings. Joanne and Kevin Nyquist think so. They are experienced travelers. They feel comfortable almost everywhere and have taken a number of trips on their own, but for their first trip to the Orient they took a Club Universe tour.

Kevin recently had a bypass operation. He's in excellent health now, but he feels that the worry and the physically trying parts of travel should be avoided. He likes the pleasure of travel, but not the work.

"All of the details Kevin usually worries about—luggage, transfers, taxis, language barriers—just disappeared," says Joanne. "The trip was quite strenuous, so it was a lifesaver having experienced people handling all the arrangements. We just sat back and enjoyed the trip."

The Nyquists haven't given up their independent travels, but when they want to explore exotic places they opt for well-conducted tours.

The American Association of Retired Persons (AARP), a nonprofit organization, has a travel service which operates exclusively for its members. As its membership numbers somewhat over 15 million, it represents a significant percentage of retired women and men. Their service offers motor-coach tours, cruises and leisure holidays in luxury apartments and major cities throughout the world. They will not organize one's personal travel itinerary, but for those who like to travel with groups, the AARP program offers a broad range of places to go at a broad range of prices—on land, on sea and by air.

There are numerous tour packages around, but retired people are missing a good bet if they don't look into tours offered by AARP.

BE A JOINER

If you don't receive at least three charter travel opportunities in the mail every year, you don't belong to enough organizations. Chances are that you do belong to a church group, a community organization, a union or a college alumni group, and that you have received those colorful brochures with pictures of tall ships, white sands and elegant hotels, but you've thrown the brochures away. Why? Because your husband's two weeks' vacation with pay never coincided with the dates of those marvelous trips to China and the Caribbean at low, low prices.

Now, you can afford to take advantage of these travel bargains because your husband's time is now his own.

Phyllis and Paul are top charter shoppers. "We're really joiners," says Phyllis. They've made it their business to join Chicago-area organizations that offer interesting trips. "Our next vacation is going to be with the Chicago Council on Foreign Relations," says Phyllis. "They offer marvelous charters. Members are interested in world affairs, so that is often the focus of the tours. We like what the Council has to offer. We attend their meetings and have met interesting people as a result. When we go on a Council charter we often know a number of people from other trips or from the meetings. What I like about these trips is that while you have much free time to go exploring on your own, there are planned events with foreign dignitaries and people in the State Department."

Think. Isn't there an organization you've been meaning to join that has a charter tour to China on its agenda?

SO WHAT'S YOUR BUDGET?
WHEN MONEY IS NO OBJECT

It cost the Hewitts $2,000 for two days aboard the Orient Express.

"It was worth it," insists Arlene. "Peter's abiding passion is trains, a fascination since childhood." When he retired from a lucrative medical practice, there was no question about what would take up the slack in Peter Hewitt's time. He has a collection of model trains, but during his medical career he didn't have enough time to indulge in his hobby.

When he retired, he promised himself and his wife,

Arlene, a wonderful vacation to celebrate their new life. He wanted to go to England—that's the hub of model train activity. Arlene opted for Italy. Since money was not a major consideration for the Hewitts, they were able to do both. The Hewitts took a train trip aboard the fabled Orient Express, starting out in England and ending in Italy. The train stops in Paris and those who wish can deboard and pick up their journey to Italy on the next run. The famous train had fallen into disrepair over the years, but today it is as luxurious as it was in its heyday.

"The restoration to its initial beauty is stunning," says Arlene. "There were no shortcuts. Every tile has been copied and replaced. Master craftsmen duplicated the original carpentry. It's a glorious feeling just to board the train and to become part of the experience of the Orient Express.

"The cars are spacious," Arlene continues. "We faced each other in luxurious chairs, with a small Victorian table between us on which to set down a cocktail, or a book, or to play Scrabble. There is a minimum dress code—jacket and tie for the men and suggested 'appropriate elegance' for the ladies. Our agent had told us you can never be overdressed on the Orient Express, and every passenger approached the journey as something special and dressed accordingly. Peter and I wore formal clothes to dinner; some of our fellow passengers even dressed in period costumes. Meals are included but ordering from the à la carte menu can run the cost up considerably. We knew before starting out that it would be costly, and we really indulged ourselves. With the extras, dinner on board the Orient Express cost us $100 per person. The first night we dined with a retired couple from New England. They were somewhat less prepared than we and ordered everything short of pigeon tongues from the à la carte menu. When the check was presented, they went into shock."

Arlene described each table as set with white linen, china, sterling silver and porcelain—all perfect copies of the original place settings.

"Sleeping aboard the Orient Express was something else," she says. "In the interest of authenticity the train does not have the shock absorbers that modern trains do, and the bumpy ride made us very aware that we were traveling.

"The bedsheets were damask, sort of a brocade material. Ashtrays, lamps and objets d'art are authentic reproductions and they are exquisite. We shopped in the boutique on board. We didn't buy anything, but it was fun looking," says Arlene.

WHEN MONEY IS THE OBJECT

If $2,000 for a two-day trip is too rich for your wallet, take a lesson from Martha and Tom Warren who, with another couple as their guests, spent a glorious weekend at a time-sharing Florida resort for a total of $49.95. "And all we had to do," says Martha, "was watch a thirty-minute promotional movie. The rest of the time was our own."

The Warrens take advantage of special weekend offers at resort hotels during the off-season. They get stays of three days and two nights for very reasonable prices. Keep an eye out for time-sharing and condo promotions. If you get on one list you are almost guaranteed to hear about every deal in town. Martha watches the newspaper ads for resort weekends. While the Warrens live in a retirement community in Florida, retirees in large cities will find posh hotels offering top accommodations and bonus meals at surprisingly low rates. A hotel weekend can be a perfect mini-vacation.

Why not take a two- or three-day trip to a county fair, community festival or outdoor art show? Go by car—it's inexpensive—and it's possible to stay at a gracious local home that offers bed and breakfast.

Short hops are a delightful break in your routine. Call or write local chambers of commerce or the state tourist bureau for information about scheduled events and for listings of private homes open to guests.

Take advantage of one-price, unlimited travel deals offered by some of the large airlines. You'll be able to visit your grandchildren in Tacoma, Washington, zip off to New York for a theater-and-restaurant holiday, and go to Florida and other destinations on the air routes of the carrier you sign on with. For example, Eastern Airlines offers unlimited travel for a year at a modest price to travelers 65 or over; a husband and wife signing up together qualify as long as one of them has reached age 65. Some major hotel chains tie in to travel packages which include air fares and room rates discounted up to 50 percent.

Discounted travel deals for men and women over retirement age are abundant for occasional trips or extensive travel plans. The growing market of travel-prone retirees has commercial carriers vying for their business, and enticing travel packages are coming on line all the time to lure the potential traveler.

BEFORE THE BIG MOVE

Vacation trips can lead to a dramatic change in your way of life. John and Pearl Richman left their Midwest home one spring and took a leisurely driving tour of the West Coast. When they reached the coast in California it was love at first sight. They checked into a hotel in Rancho Santa Fe, stayed two weeks and bought their retirement home before they left.

"It was pure impulse," says Pearl, "but when we saw the lovely flowers, the blue Pacific, the rolling terrain, it was too much. We started house hunting at once and found the house we could afford." When the Richmans returned to the Midwest they put their house up for sale and made plans to make the permanent move to their new home in California.

"We had talked about the possibility of moving west to be closer to our children and grandchildren who live in Oregon. But we never really talked about it seriously. Our trip to California was the turning point.

Even though we still are a distance from the children, it is closer. At least we're in the same time zone, and we will get to see the little ones more often."

If you and your husband have talked about the possibility of spending your retirement years in the dry weather and sunshine of Tucson, Arizona, or on the west coast of Florida enjoying the gulf breezes, or at Leisure Village in California where retirees are the leading citizens, we recommend a vacation trip there to test the waters. You might find the constant sunshine boring. You might find your arthritis kicks up in damp climates. You might find that life in a small community isn't as stimulating as life in the big city where you live now. But, then again, you might find that life in the Sun Belt is what you've always dreamed it would be—perfect. If it works out that way you'll be ready for the Big Move (see Chapter 7).

*R*OUGHING IT

Betty and Stan Kaplan always thought they would like to hit the open road—become campers. But they weren't sure that life in a motor home was for them. "We took a trial run," says Betty. "We rented a Winnebago and took off on our first camping trip." The Kaplans traveled from Florida to Arizona, and they now spend six months out of the year in their very own Winnebago.

They joined a national motor-home organization and subscribed to at least three publications devoted to cross-country motoring. The Kaplans leave their chilly midwestern hometown every year after Thanksgiving and head south or west, or in whichever direction the caravan excursion they have chosen is going. One year they joined a group of sixty-five other motor-home owners in Texas and, armed with their CB radios, 140 hardy souls set out for a six-week Mexican adventure. They were led by a wagon master whose Mexican-born wife seemed to have a close relative to welcome them in every small town south of the border.

"One evening, after we had settled in the trailer park, the wagon master broke off from the rest of the group and headed to town for supplies. A few miles out he looked back to find four vans obediently following him! It's not exactly a spontaneous kind of travel," says Betty.

"We've discovered a cross section of the country we didn't really know the first sixty years of our lives. It was no big decision to give up those bridge games, luncheons and dinner parties at home for life on the road. And we've made so many new friends. At the end of the day there is a get-together of the entire caravan at a prearranged campsite for an evening barbecue or a square dance. It helps if at least one of you has a gregarious nature—some people can make lasting friendships as they are hooking up the water supply."

Is joining a caravan of motor homes driving cross-country expensive? Yes and no. Most motor homes don't get more than ten miles to a gallon of gas, which can add up at the end of a day of driving. On the other hand, the Kaplans' six-week trip to Mexico included entertainment each evening, docking space and the services of a wagon master for only $300. Should you find a favorite vacation spot that you want to return to on a regular basis, you can buy a permanent slot to park your van.

"Of course, whenever you travel it helps to be in good health," says Betty. "But we have seen people who have suffered the effects of arthritis or even stroke join the caravans. Either the husband or wife takes on all the driving. It's a way to enjoy travel and still have the convenience of home. We've seen the country close up at a fraction of the cost of using commercial transportation. Since we cook our own meals we don't have the expense of having to eat out in restaurants three times a day."

So What If It Doesn't Work Out?

Seeing the country in a recreational van sounded like a great postretirement project to Michelle and Bill Morris. Michelle was only lukewarm about the idea at first, but Bill's enthusiasm was contagious. During his last year in the family business, Bill bought a van and spent every spare hour in the garage converting it into comfortably condensed living quarters, and one day after his retirement they set off on a 4,000-mile tour of state parks and historic sites of the eastern United States.

"We spent a total of three nights on the trip sleeping in the van," says Michelle. "It was culture shock. We had always traveled in a conventional way, staying at recommended hotels, and that's what we ended up doing. We would drive to the points of interest on our itinerary each day, park the van and register at the best hotel in town each evening. We loved the trip, but it taught us a camper's life is not for us. When we returned home, our first act was to put the van up for sale and then we sat down to plan our next trip—around the world on standby."

Camping out is an ideal travel activity for many but it doesn't suit everyone. The Morrises might have been wiser to rent an RV instead of buying one, but even so they were willing to risk the adventure. So what if your travel plans don't always work out the way you expect. You'll have some terrific stories to tell when you get home.

Be Your Own Agent

"Traveling is something we both enjoy," says Barbara Townsend. "In the past it was Carl who set the dates and planned the trips and made sure we got away regularly. Now that we're in the travel business we're partners, and we do all of our travel planning together."

After Carl Townsend retired, he heard about a half partnership in a travel agency for sale in his hometown of Cleveland. He and Barbara talked it over and decided to invest in the agency in order to indulge in their fantasy of unlimited travel opportunities. "We both thought it would be a great way to travel in style— a chance to go everywhere and make a little money on the side," says Barbara.

"Carl had been in the plastics business; my working experience had been as a dress designer, sometime interior decorator and consultant for the college collection at a Cleveland department store. With this wonderful wealth of experience we led a group of twenty-five innocents who had answered an ad in the *Cleveland Press* for a Mediterranean tour. I was assigned the job of treasurer, with duties that included luggage counting, dispensing aspirin, Lomotil and Band-Aids.

"Off we set for the Mediterranean, with a long stopover in the Greek Islands—then to Lisbon, Madrid and Toledo. In a small town in Spain one of our passengers had a heart attack; there were few English-speaking people around at this time. My own command of Spanish was limited to such conversational gambits as 'My aunt's umbrella is black.' Not much help in a medical emergency. We managed to get our sick lady bedded down in a local hospital, located her family in the States, and I waited for them while Carl went on with the troops. When her children arrived, and I knew she was out of danger, I caught up with the tour.

"As we became more knowledgeable," Barbara continued, "we discovered that the most satisfying tours for us were those sponsored by companies or organizations that brought people with a shared interest together. The General Electric Company had retirement benefits in their employee package that included wonderful group trips. We have taken many trips with G.E. retirees—to the Orient, Europe and Egypt. While the G.E. people come from all over the country, many are Cleveland-based and remain our good friends to this day.

"The real perks of being a part-time travel agent are the special trips we take on our own at minimal cost. As agents we went first-class all the way on the British liner *Queen Elizabeth II* at one quarter the price, and we were treated like royalty."

Carol Fletcher, who lives in Palm Springs, California, enjoys the perks of travel agenting as well. She works out of her home, writes up tickets and makes reservations for her friends and neighbors and goes to the office only when she has to. She's getting ready to take a one-week cruise to Alaska—a freebie!

Sue Simon became a part-time travel agent at about the same time her husband, Burt, retired. Her business has steadily increased, and now she goes to the office almost every day. Burt has encouraged her; he has added to Sue's clientele by making contacts with old business associates, and together they enjoy reduced fares and special trips to Europe and the Orient.

Both Sue and Carol, now that they are in the travel business, have taken off on trips alone.

GOING TO TRAVEL ON YOUR OWN?

You love to travel; your husband tolerates it. He would much rather spend warm, sunny days on the golf course than in airports or on the road. At least that's the way Carol Fletcher's husband, Art, feels. When Carol was first offered a one-week cruise to Alaska as part of a travel promotion, she asked Art to join her. "He really doesn't want to go, so I'm going by myself. I've taken short trips on my own before. It's good for both of us. I'm never away too long and it gives us a chance to miss each other," she says.

Carol wasn't the only one interviewed who enjoys traveling alone. Ellen takes short trips to visit her children or her old college roommates. Emily takes long weekends with her grandchildren. Their husbands don't seem to mind, each preferring to stay home and follow his own pursuits.

Emily and Martin Shuman do like to travel. "Our long trips are always together," says Emily. "We went to Europe last year, and I often spend four or five days away, never more, on my own. Martin encourages me to take an occasional trip without him, and I think it's good for both of us."

It does seem that women have more wanderlust than men—at least the women we interviewed did—and many managed to take solo trips successfully. A few of them felt guilty about it. Joanne Nyquist, who took a visiting sister on a tour of southern California, made several frozen dinners for Kevin, neatly marking them with cooking instructions. "I don't know why I bothered. They were still in the freezer when I got home," says Joanne. "Kevin had gone out for dinner with friends almost every night that I was gone."

If your husband prefers home to hotels, must you deny yourself an occasional trip? Absolutely not. We don't suggest that you plan the Grand Tour of Europe or go around the world in eighty days, but most husbands don't object when their wives take brief vacations on their own.

If you are going to travel without him, it is important that you not feel guilty. You aren't abandoning your husband; you are simply following an interest of your own. If you act guilty, he'll probably pick up on the cue and start to think that you have done something wrong. It goes without saying that if you go to your college reunion by yourself, or take a week off and go to a spa, you can't pout when he decides to go fishing with three of his men friends.

IN CASE OF ILLNESS

Before you set out on your trip to visit a neighboring city, to see the U.S.A. or to go around the world, take a few basic health precautions.

Margaret and Dan Roth travel frequently, despite his cardiac condition. Margaret has a checklist she calls her "personal health insurance" that she claims is as important as a valid passport and her Berlitz book of *Language for Travelers.*

Margaret packs enough prescription medicine for the entire trip. She also carries a duplicate set of prescriptions; proof of medical need can allay the suspicions of an overzealous customs inspector, and the prescriptions may turn out to be a lifesaver for emergency refills. She carries a strip of Dan's last cardiogram as a basis of comparison should he have a health problem during the trip. The name, address and phone number of their physician is clipped to the Roths' passport, as is the name and phone number of their son, Michael.

Margaret updates her list of English-speaking physicians who practice in the countries they plan to visit. The Roths subscribe to the International Association for Medical Assistance to Travelers (IAMAT) which publishes a reference directory of English-speaking doctors worldwide.* "The language barrier is our number one concern when either of us feels ill on a trip," claims Margaret. "Describing your ailment to an uncomprehending doctor or nurse can be enough to set off a chain reaction of tension, frustration and dangerous misunderstanding. I learned my lesson during a trip to Spain where I became ill with a persistent cold and cough. The hotel had a physician on call who prescribed medication—an antibiotic I thought—and we continued our itinerary, I, confident the miracle drug was working all the time I was playing. It wasn't until I returned home that I discovered I had pneumonia, and the 'antibiotic' I had been taking was a Spanish aspirin mixture."

The hotel concierge, the American consul, an IAMAT-recommended physician are all people you can

---

*IAMAT-recommended doctors charge on a set payment scale. To receive the directory, it is suggested you send a $20 contribution to the organization. For information, write: IAMAT, 736 Center Street, Lewiston, New York 14092

turn to in case of emergency illness while abroad. You can help them help you by carrying information about your medical history with you. You might also consider joining the Medic Alert Foundation,* which keeps your medical history on file, is on call worldwide twenty-four hours a day, can communicate in several languages and has a toll-free phone number.

RULES OF THE ROAD

We've probably convinced you that travel and retirement are synonymous, but before you call your travel agent, or try to become one, we suggest that you and your husband make an appointment with each other. Travel is one activity that should be planned together from the very start.

Remember these steps when making travel plans with your retired husband:

• *Talk to him.* Unless you tell him what your travel interests are and he expresses his, there's going to be friction—particularly when you've booked him on a tour of the Great Wall of China and he wants to go fishing in Eagle River, Wisconsin.

• *Compromise.* We don't mean do what he wants to do at all times. But be willing to give fishing a try if he will venture forth on that trip to the Orient.

• *Plan together.* Researching a trip, making arrangements, choosing hotels, talking to agents can be as much fun as the trip itself. If you're planning a trip to London, stake out the areas each of you wants to investigate. You might want to look into theater offerings and side trips into the countryside.

---

* To join Medic Alert write: Medic Alert Foundation International, P.O. Box 1009, Turlock, California 95381.

For a $15 fee, you can become a lifetime member of Medic Alert. After completing a medical information form, you will receive a silver tag with your identification number and your pertinent vital medical information, such as a penicillin allergy or the presence of a heart pacemaker.

He might want to look into military museums and antique shops.

• *Budget the trip.* This must be a joint project. If you figure the costs together, then you can talk about what extra money is left for fine dining and shopping. It saves wear and tear later on. You each might want to have a separate but equal amount of money to spend on shopping, or perhaps you are art lovers and intend to make a single but meaningful purchase on this trip.

• *Risk adventure.* At the risk of repeating ourselves, let us say that retirement is one door closing and another one opening. Go through that door. Allow the unexpected to happen. It's the unanticipated adventure, the new people you meet, the little restaurant you discover that's not in any guidebook, that make the trip worthwhile.

5
SHE WORKS, HE DOESN'T

*We wouldn't be destitute if I
quit my job. But I enjoy the
extra money and, even more,
I enjoy the satisfaction I get
from my work.*
Phyllis Foreman

When Sharon Cooper announced to her friends
at lunch one day that her husband was going
to retire before the end of the year, she laughed self-
consciously and said, "When he retires, I think I'm
going to get a job." Sharon was being funny. Certainly
her friends knew that she didn't mean it. The truth is
that Sharon had never held a paying job. She had spent
all thirty-five years of her marriage as a housewife and
mother and liked her life. But when questioned further
Sharon admitted that she was apprehensive about her
husband's staying home all of the time. Perhaps, she
mused, it *was* time for her to get out in the world.

If you aren't employed already, it's a good bet that
since your husband is about to retire or has retired,
you've toyed with the notion of getting a job yourself.
It's not a farfetched idea. There are at least four major
reasons why women want to work after their husbands
retire:

1. They derive self-esteem from their work.
2. They add to limited retirement incomes and their jobs often provide much-needed health benefits.
3. They enjoy the intellectual stimulation and social contacts their jobs bring.
4. They get away from the responsibility of their houses and too much togetherness with their spouses.

SELF-ESTEEM

How many times have you been at a gathering and by way of introduction a person will ask, "What do you do?" Do you grit your teeth, swallow your pride and answer, "I don't do anything; I'm just a housewife"? Or are you one of those for whom being a successful home-maker is a recognizable accomplishment of which you are justifiably proud? Unfortunately attending to the day-to-day tasks of making a home just doesn't have the cachet of a paying job.

It isn't written anywhere that only men enjoy the recognition that comes with success in their chosen fields. Working women like the identity their jobs give them. Asked "What do you do?" a number of the wives of retirees we talked to were quick to answer: "I teach fifth grade at a school for gifted children"; "I treat emotionally disturbed adolescents"; "I teach French at the University of Illinois"; "I'm vice president in charge of marketing for a major corporation"; "I've done Mrs. Frank Sinatra's nails." It's apparent from their answers that these women get ego satisfaction from the work they do.

Jill Holder is a family psychotherapist and her office is in her home. Although she's 65, her practice is still growing and sometimes her appointments start as early as seven in the morning. She's a handsome, energetic woman who loves her work and knows she was lucky to have found such a satisfying career at a time most of her friends were opting for a house in the suburbs and volunteer work.

"I'll never stop working; it's in the genes. My mother is 88, had a stroke and lives in a nursing home, but she still bets on the horses—and wins!"

Jill was widowed at 31. She returned to school, became a psychotherapist and had an established practice before she married Alex Holder ten years later. "My first husband's death made me take stock of my life," she says. "I realized that if I felt I was a victim I would become one. If I'm only somebody's parent I will get fired from that job one day, and *then* who will I be? And if I'm only Alex's wife, that limits me, too."

Since Jill's job is so important to her, she was particularly empathetic when her husband, Alex, retired from business four years ago. "I see so many couples professionally who are going through the retirement experience," says Jill. "There's a stress factor in any loss, and giving up a business you were successful in is a personal loss. It took about six or eight months for Alex to find his new self, but I think the most important thing is that we talked out loud about it. We agreed I would continue my career and that we would accommodate our new life together around my working schedule."

Alex has found a number of activities that keep him on the go when Jill is working. He has adopted a school where he tutors slow readers and helps with an after-school recreational program.

Occasionally Jill accepts speaking engagements out of the city. If the destination is one that appeals to both of them, they build a vacation out of it. She is able to enjoy the self-esteem her work gives her because her relationship with Alex is solid and he doesn't mind basking in her reflected glory.

Jane Avery is vice president and marketing director of a Fortune 500 company, and her husband is retired. At work she has a large, bright corner office in a new downtown building. There's a carpet on the floor and her name is on the door. During a recent two-week hospital stay for surgery, she didn't complain about the frequent phone calls from her office each day. They were constant reminders that she was important and that she was missed, and it was good medicine for her morale.

At home, Jane shares her personal life with husband Leonard, a former lamp manufacturer who sold his business and retired at age 55. "Leonard is a wonderful companion to me," she says. "He understands that I've reached the peak of my career at this time and that I savor it. It was when Len had to drive me to work after I returned from the hospital, and then had to do the marketing and make the meals, that he became morose.

"He never should have retired," she reflects. "What he really needed was a sabbatical from work. Once he left his job he just never got involved in anything that held a real interest for him, and he says retirement was the worst thing in the world.

"I'd like to help him but he's going to have to find something productive to do on his own." She paused. "I'm not ready to give up my job."

SOCIAL AND INTELLECTUAL STIMULATION

On the first day of Roy Bowles's retirement as chief operating officer of his small manufacturing company, his wife Norma made him his breakfast, led him to the refrigerator, pointed to the ham and cheese for his luncheon sandwich and headed out of the door to her first class at Northwestern University.

"Our two daughters were away at school, Roy was happy to be home, and I was definitely ready for a change of scenery," says Norma, who needed a few courses to finish her degree. After graduation she got a job teaching math at the junior college level.

"I knew that if Roy was going to be home all day I

had to get out and do something. Too much being together is not a good thing," she explains. "If a couple is together all of the time and shares every experience there isn't much left to talk about." Norma feels that by going to work when Roy retired she enriched their relationship. She likes the intellectual stimulation from colleagues and students during her teaching day, then looks forward to the evening with Roy and sharing the day's news over dinner.

Norma has a quick mind and many interests. She is a professional weaver and has shown her work in several exhibitions. One day a week she teaches weaving, and she has made friends with fellow artists. She feels strongly that a woman makes a mistake when she allows her husband's retirement to curtail her activities.

"I have a friend who is extremely bright," says Norma. "She was involved in a number of projects that used her talents, but when her husband retired, she felt guilty about leaving him and she withdrew from her pursuits as well. It really is unfortunate."

Norma doesn't feel guilty about leaving Roy. He has some real estate interests that he handles from his office at home, and she feels that he is more than capable of taking care of his own time. "I do see that his lunch is made. I have a repertoire of simple meals that I freeze, and all Roy has to do is put them in the microwave." Norma is proud that she finally got him to make his own breakfast because she is on her way to work when he is ready for his morning meal. She laughs. "Roy has made the same breakfast every day since he retired all those years ago. He likes it that way and so do I."

Norma is convinced that their married life is better because of the outside intellectual stimulation in her life. She does admit that Roy sometimes hates to see her go. "When I'm on my way to the Weavers' Guild meeting or to an appointment, he will think of something he has to tell me or something he wants me to do; I don't mind, but I'm usually about ten minutes late to wherever I'm going."

*S*OCIAL CONTACTS

"It's a chance to be with people who have become my closest friends," says Betsy Dawes. Betsy is a manicurist whose husband, Ed, has retired. They live in a mobile home in what is primarily a retirement community in Palm Springs. Betsy works in an attractive beauty salon whose owner, Beth Jordan, is her best friend. The salon is successful, with a staff of about eight people who share a real camaraderie. In addition, Betsy, a woman in her middle fifties, has made fast friendships with clients. "I would miss my job terribly if I had to quit," she says. Fortunately Ed is not threatened by Betsy's devotion to her work. "He does call me at work at least once a day, but it's usually to see how I am or to share something that happened to him. He doesn't overdo it, and I want him to know he can keep in touch with me while I'm working."

Perhaps the wisest thing Betsy does is include Ed in her work-related social life. When her colleagues have a party, Ed is invited. He goes with the group on its annual outing to Las Vegas, and recently Ed joined Betsy and the rest of the salon staff at a business convention in Los Angeles. "Ed enjoyed the week there," says Betsy. "He gets along well with everyone, and we were together even though I was doing something connected with my work."

If you're like Norma or Betsy, you probably have a good sense of who you are. You love your husband, try to see to his needs, and are, in a sense, his best friend, but you also have to have a life of your own that is creative and stimulating. A job may be just what you need. Working outside your home will keep your brain cells active and will widen your contacts with other people. Best of all, it can increase the vitality of your marriage.

SHE BRINGS HOME THE PAYCHECK

Katherine Heller enjoys the challenge of her job as a social worker, and she likes the interaction with other people that her workday brings, but the bottom line is that Katherine works because she and her husband need the money. She is the family breadwinner since husband Paul retired. Paul sold his marginal data processing business when he was only 52 years old. Katherine assumed Paul would get a job to supplement their inadequate retirement income, but as she explains: "Paul loves being home. He is willing to cook, clean and shop and somehow he never got around to looking for work." Katherine's income as well as the health benefits she receives in her job are a necessity for the Hellers.

The majority of working women interviewed did so to provide for the "extras"—the things that make life more fun. Betsy Dawes, the manicurist, not only likes the social contacts her work gives her but appreciates the extra money as well. Last year she banked a good part of her salary, lived carefully on Ed's modest retirement income and then popped for a Caribbean cruise. "It was everything I dreamed it would be," says Betsy, who hasn't had an opportunity to travel a great deal. She's saving for a trip to Hawaii now.

One of Mary Sullivan's greatest joys is sending her grandchildren their Easter outfits or providing her married children with little luxuries they cannot afford. Mary makes a modest salary in a part-time job in a local bookstore. "It's probably psychological," she says. "I really don't make that much, but I feel less guilty about being a bit frivolous with money because I know I am contributing something to the family income."

IT'S A WAY TO GET AWAY

There are women who feel more comfortable leaving their retired husbands if they are going off to do something productive, and in our society a job is productive. Call it the work ethic, but we all feel better about ourselves when we are engaged in useful activity.

We've already agreed that even a couple whose marriage is idyllic and who love to share their every experience still have to have time apart. If you find that you suffer from the guilts every time you leave your husband to go off and play bridge with your friends, yet still feel the need to have some time apart, getting a full- or part-time job may be just the way to legitimize your need for some separateness.

"I thought we would do some traveling when Grant retired, and I even considered quitting my job. Instead he has become a real house husband." Louise Wescott sighs. "I actually look forward to going to work on Monday mornings. When I'm home on the weekends Grant expects me to share his every enthusiasm. A weekend with Grant can be exhausting."

Louise's husband took to his retirement with the zest of a young man. He did not miss his job as a city policeman for one minute. He is a gourmet cook, raises tropical fish, paneled the family room in their house and built a grape arbor in their backyard, intending to use his harvest to make jams, jellies and his brand of wine.

Louise has a good civil service job. When she gets home in the evening, Grant has dinner made. "He has a whole group of men friends who retired at about the same time," she says. "They spend their afternoons together and they have become real gossips. You think women are bad—you should hear the juicy stories Grant has to tell me when I get home at night. He knows more about what's going on in the neighborhood than I did when I was home raising the children!"

Like Louise's story, but with a twist, is the experience of Donna Fox. She has a part-time job that keeps her out of her home three days a week. She likes her work in the personnel department of a large university. But to tell the truth, she would quit in a minute if her husband, Perry, didn't want *her* out of the house.

Donna is a warm, good-humored woman who seems to understand her husband's need for privacy. "You see, he has always been interested in the theater and he looked forward to retirement as a time when he would write a play, and that's just what he is doing," she says. "When I'm home I have a tendency to interrupt him, or the phone rings for me too many times, and he finds that he just can't concentrate, so I give him his space when I go off to work."

Perry is content having his wife work and is enjoying doing some of the household tasks that used to be hers. Perry, like the husbands of a number of women interviewed, was not threatened by role reversal.

PROBLEMS OF ROLE REVERSAL

Before you start poring over the want ads or knocking on the doors of employment agencies, you'd better be aware of one major problem you might face as the only employed member of your household:

You have a good marriage.

You love him.

He loves you.

However, since your husband has retired and you are working, he seems resentful of your job-related interests. Or, perhaps, he enjoys your bringing home that paycheck and you find yourself steaming inside when he tells you how it's going to be spent. Both of you are having trouble with your sudden reversal of traditional roles.

An extensive study on the psychological changes in women and men in the course of the aging process, conducted at Northwestern University under the direction of Dr. Jerome Grunes, concludes that by the time a man reaches late middle age he is inclined to turn from his managerial tendencies to a need to be nurtured. A woman at the same age tends to move to greater activity—to have a new sense of self that didn't have a chance to blossom in her earlier, mothering years. Says Dr. Grunes, "She wants the opportunity now to be self-exploratory. At the same time she will be reacting to the shift in her husband from the warrior phase of bringing home the bear meat, to his patriarch phase of sitting at the head of the tribe dealing out sage advice."

All would be well if you and your husband felt the need to reverse roles at the very same time, but such transitions are not always simultaneous or smooth.

Look what happened to Phyllis Foreman.

SOMEBODY AT WORK—NOBODY AT HOME

Phyllis Foreman, whose husband, Dan, is a retired executive, is head of the occupational therapy department of a large rehabilitation center. When her children went to college, she returned to school, acquired her credentials and became recognized for her expertise in her field. She has served on a governmental commission and often gives lectures to other professionals. In short, she's a success. "I really look forward to going to work," says Phyllis.

On a typical working day she rises early, puts up the coffee, makes the bed while her retired husband has breakfast, and then heads for the 7:55 train to the city. She arrives at the center where she puts in a full and fulfilling day. Then it's back to her suburban home on the 5:08. When she enters the house, her husband greets her with those immortal words: "What's for dinner?"

Phyllis feels that she's *somebody* at work. "But at home Dan never directly acknowledges that what I do is important or even that I'm helping out financially," she complains.

"While he worked Dan made a good living. We lived conservatively and made good investments. We wouldn't be destitute if I quit my job. But I enjoy the extra money and, even more, I enjoy the satisfaction I get from my work."

With all the recognition she gets at her job, Phyllis still smarts from what she feels is a lack of appreciation at home. "He wants to call all the shots. On weekends and the several paid holidays I get during the year, he assumes we will spend the entire time together. I never feel free to stay for office get-togethers or accept out-of-town invitations to speak because it's not worth seeing him sulk."

Phyllis thinks Dan diminishes what she does. "He'll laugh and say, 'You can buy your groceries on your pension when you retire.' Well, I don't intend to retire!" she insists.

Phyllis wishes her husband would find something to occupy him so she wouldn't feel so guilty about enjoying the work she does. "He really can write well. I thought maybe he could write a book. But he doesn't want to do anything—he just doesn't have any ambition!"

Phyllis isn't giving Dan any more appreciation than he is giving her. Her complaint about his lack of ambition is ironic. Dan Foreman had worked hard all of his life and provided well. He was a top executive with a barrel and drum company but he found himself jobless at age 60 when the cooperage was sold to a large conglomerate. "He spent a couple of months looking around for something," Phyllis says, "but he was only interested in a position at the executive level and soon got the message that he was not marketable because of his age." It wasn't long before Dan gave up the search altogether and considered himself retired from his working life.

At the same time that her work was giving Phyllis a sense of identity, Dan's retirement was robbing him of his. If Phyllis feels unappreciated at home, Dan feels unappreciated by the world at large. He can't accept the role reversal.

We talked earlier about Katherine Heller, who became the chief money-maker in her family after her husband, Paul, retired. Katherine reflected some of the confusion that many women feel who contribute necessary financial aid to the family. She loves her job as a social worker but nevertheless resents Paul's being home enjoying himself. She knows that he spent years doing his share, but now that she is bringing home the paycheck she feels frustrated and angry. "I don't like feeling that I have no options," complains Katherine. "If Paul went back to work, I could quit my job if I wanted to." Does she want to quit? Would she quit if she could? The answer is no. Katherine knows she sounds a bit mixed-up. "I guess I'm used to men being the support of their families."

What really bothers Katherine is the role reversal that has taken place in her family. She insists that her 21-year-old son is embarrassed because his mother works and his father does many of the household chores, but it is *Katherine* who worries about what people think. The tension between the Hellers seems to be mounting. He says he will go back to work if the opportunity comes along, but he doesn't seem to be looking too hard.

Katherine and Paul drifted into their situation. They have not done a good job of communicating their feelings to each other, and Katherine, despite her intelligence and the importance of her job, is still hung up on what she sees as appropriate roles for men and women. She doesn't feel at ease with the fact that they have somewhat reversed roles.

WHERE DOES HER MONEY GO?

"The way I feel is that the money Jack makes is ours and the money I make is mine," says Margaret Phillips, who makes about ten thousand dollars a year as a free-lance photographer. Her husband likes it that way, too. Margaret puts most of her money into a money fund, but with the rest she buys clothes that are a bit more expensive and doesn't feel guilty about it. She even indulges Jack with an occasional gift for no reason at all.

Not so with the Volpes. Bernard Volpe has always handled all of the finances in the family. He runs a tight ship, and Agnes has had to ask for money for special or unexpected expenditures. Bernard has not ever been generous. When Agnes started to make some money on her own, catering fancy desserts from her home, she turned her checks over to her husband for deposit in their bank account. Despite the fact that the account is in both their names, Agnes does not feel free to write a check on it unless she clears it with her husband. She is unhappy with the situation and yet she doesn't seem to know how to change it. To this day, even though Agnes earns money each year, she has to clear all spending with Bernard.

Once you become a wage earner, you'll have to decide how to handle your income. Every family works out its financial structure differently. Make sure you and your husband talk about your contribution to the family income. Most of the couples interviewed *did* work out a constructive method of spending their money. Most often the wife's income meant the addition of little and even big luxuries. Sometimes her income is an absolute necessity. Whatever your case happens to be, be sure that you and your husband decide together how it will be handled. Purse strings that are too tightly pulled by either husband or wife can have a strangling effect on a relationship.

MIXED FEELINGS

If your husband has mixed feelings about your going to work, try to find out what really bothers him about the idea.

There is one good reason why he might not be thrilled with your ambitions for a new career. Remember, retirement means freedom for him. At last he can travel—

take off for a day, a week, a month—whenever he wants to, and he wants *you* to be with him. Be flattered by his desire to be with you, and then try to find a comfortable compromise.

Terry Smitz feels she's found a satisfactory solution. She is a full-time librarian but didn't take the job until she was assured that she could take a two-week winter vacation and a two-week summer vacation. Since she works a five-day week, she and her husband take weekend trips throughout the year as well. Marge Spiro, whom you will meet later, gave up her full-time job for a free-lance job in order to spend more time with her husband, but she did keep working.

Perhaps your husband has a deeper, more complex reason for not wanting you to work. The role reversal—he stays home, you go to the office—might be too difficult for him to take. His masculinity is threatened. He wants you home at his side. It's up to you to decide what you want to do if you know this is the situation. If you can stay home happily fulfilled with your life together, fine. But it would be unwise to martyr yourself, to give up your aspirations and stay home just to soothe his ego. You'd feel frustrated and angry in no time. You've reached that stage in your life when you have to do what satisfies you. You've been the nurturer; now you want to retire from that job and take another.

Tell your husband why a job is important to you and assure him that he has your love and your respect; then head for that personnel office. You'll probably put up with some pouting at first, but he will adjust. You'll be a lot easier to live with if you're doing what you want to do.

So YOU'RE GOING TO WORK

You and your husband have talked over his upcoming retirement and you agree that the new-found time together will be wonderful, but that some time apart will make it even more valued. He's looking forward to time at home. You've often thought of expanding your horizons, and now you decide to go back to work for one, two, three or even five days a week.

If you are thinking about getting a job, here are some suggestions that might be helpful:

• *Prepare a resume.* Even if you never have the need to submit a formal resume to a prospective employer, preparing one will help you evaluate your own potential. List your working experience, community involvement, education. It is neither necessary nor advisable to list your date of birth or marital status. You are selling your ability; the latter information is not necessarily relevant to the skills you can bring to a job and may prejudice your opportunity for employment.

• *Upgrade your skills.* You may want to take a brush-up course in typing or, better still, a short course in word processing or other computer-based skills. There's a sure market for people able to work with state-of-the-art equipment, and it can guarantee your entry into the job market.

• *Dust off your diploma.* Do you have a teaching degree? Investigate ways you can put it to work. A degree in education can qualify you as a substitute teacher in your local school system. You can say yes or no when you are called for work without jeopardizing future work assignments, and the pay is good. At the secondary school level your bachelor's degree with a major in math, English or science may be enough to get you on the payroll as a substitute teacher. There are a number of innovative programs specifically directed to hard-to-reach, hard-to-teach children. Your teaching degree, your own life experience and supplemental courses in psychology and education can prepare you for an exciting teaching position.

• *Capitalize on your interests.* Were you the treasurer of your book club? Ruth Bellows was. She did such a good job that the group leader asked her to handle the scheduling and bookkeeping for other book clubs, for a percentage. Are you an expert knitter or weaver? A neighborhood crafts shop might be looking for someone just like you to work part-time.

• *Do you volunteer at the art museum?* You might be able to get a paying job at an art gallery.

• *Try networking.* Make a list of friends and acquaintances who own businesses or have jobs with organizations that sound interesting to you. Write a brief note asking for advice to those people you believe might be responsive and follow up in a few days with a phone call. If you are able to make a date to discuss the job hunt with your friend, fine. If your contact is not receptive, accept the turndown graciously and go on to the next name on your list. Tell everyone you know of your desire and availability for work. Some banks have part-time employment programs for people 55 and over; you might check with yours. The important thing is to use your imagination *and* use your personal address book. You never know where the perfect job is waiting for you.

• *Apply to senior employment centers.* Believe it or not, there are companies that *prefer* to hire mature workers. Older-worker organizations such as Operation ABLE (Ability Based on Long Experience) are now located in such cities as Chicago, Boston, Little Rock, San Francisco, Los Angeles and New York and are devoted solely to matching over-55 job seekers with employers. You might want to check with the senior center in your community. The Winnetka Senior Center in Winnetka, Illinois, has an excellent employment service.

PART-TIME WORK/FREE-LANCE WORK

We've talked about substitute teaching, which permits you flexible schedules and options. But there are also working arrangements that permit you to hold down a responsible job and have your play time, too. Donna Fox has worked out a job-sharing arrangement with the wife of another retired civil servant in her home town of Washington, D.C. Her employers at the university are pleased with the schedule Donna and her partner have devised. They work alternately the first four days of the week and work together on Fridays.

Pat Skidmore works in a local bookstore three days a week. Retail stores, particularly in suburban malls, are often in the market for part-time sales help. Check the ads in your neighborhood newspaper or suburban weekly for part-time jobs close to home.

Free-lance work which you can do in your own home and on your own time can fit in perfectly with your new lifestyle. Marjorie Spiro testifies to that. Marjorie had worked during most of her marriage. "My resume is quite impressive," she says, "and at the age of 50 I commanded top dollar as a publicist and development director for a charitable foundation."

Then her husband, Tom, retired. He plays first violin in a community orchestra, he goes to all the art gallery openings and has a box for the Chicago Cubs baseball season. Marge, tied to her nine-to-five workday, watched her husband enjoy his happy retirement and then reassessed her priorities. Her going-away party at the office was lovely.

She now writes annual reports and edits the company house organ on her own time. And she's with her husband rooting for the Cubs at all the home games.

What are your skills? Typing? Sewing? Knitting? Cooking? Wendy bakes her private-recipe cheesecakes for a well-known catering firm in her own kitchen.

If you work at home, be sure to have your own space to work, and make sure you and your husband agree that your work time is your own.

*A*RE YOU A VOLUNTEER?

It may be a volunteer job but it's still a job. There are people who look on volunteers as social butterflies or do-gooders. But we know volunteer work is serious business. We don't have to tell you how hard volunteers work or how significant their jobs are because chances are you are at a stage in life in which you already have been involved with volunteer work.

Lois Casey is an excellent example of a woman who finds meaning in volunteer work. Her husband is a retired member of the State Department. Since he was a career diplomat, Lois found herself traveling all over the world. She has resided in Lisbon, Oslo, Paris, Rio and Mexico City. "Each time we moved, I was forced to make new friends and get involved in the community," says Lois. The diplomat's life is not all teas and receptions. Lois found that raising her five children and doing volunteer work in each community in which they lived was the best way to get to know people.

"I used exactly the same method of getting acquainted after Bill retired," Lois explains. "We chose to live in Connecticut because we found a lovely community there. But we knew no one. After we settled in, I did what I have always done when I came to any new place: I looked into volunteer opportunities. I work three days a week as a teacher's aide. My work is with children who are having difficulty with math and science. I really love children; I have five of my own, and I feel at ease with them. I've met quite a few people and have made several good friends."

Whatever your reasons for working after your husband retires, be aware that there will be an adjustment in your domestic life. You will make the best accommodation to the revised roles in your marriage if the two of your talk about it. Together, explore the advantages of your working. Try to anticipate possible problems. Above all, be honest with yourself. Understand your motives for working, be sensitive to your job's effect on your marriage and then rate the priorities in your life.

6
FRICTION
OVER
FINANCES

*I don't think Frank would
mind my buying a mink coat,
but he will argue with me for
not buying a generic brand
of pickles.*

Sara Leland

Y ou and your husband are looking forward to retirement. You both think of it as a beginning. You know where you're going to live; you have plans for activities you will pursue; you've mapped some trips you're going to take. You've talked about everything— but have you talked about money?

If the subject of money was a source of tension before your husband's retirement, think of the friction money can cause now that you are going to be on a fixed income. We're not suggesting that money *has* to be a problem. Most retirees today are fairly secure, thanks to pension plans, investments and Social Security. Chances are retired husbands know pretty much what their situations are. But all too often the wives of retirees have only a vague idea of their finances, and just the thought of living without that regular paycheck looms as a frightening prospect.

Jill Peters is a good example. Her husband will be retiring in three months. He has planned carefully for his retirement, and deep down Jill knows that he has, but she confesses she is frightened. "Just the thought of living on a fixed income makes me nervous," says Jill. "I've already told my married children not to expect any more expensive gifts. And something strange is happening to me. I suddenly have more wants—not needs, wants. I never was a compulsive shopper; now that I know we are going to be on a fixed income, I want to go shopping all of the time. I don't understand what is happening to me!"

The availability of enough money to live comfortably, whatever your established lifestyle, is basic to a successful retirement. Even if you do have enough money, you do not have a guarantee that there will not be friction over finances.

Whether you and your husband are entering your retirement life on a modest but adequate income or you're one of the lucky couples retiring on a large income, *you must talk about money.* If you don't, you might find yourself in the Volpes' situation.

WHO HOLDS THE PURSE STRINGS?

Agnes Volpe used to plan her life around her husband, Bernard. He had always been the dominant member in their relationship. She ran her household to please him and he made all of their financial decisions. Agnes said that once Bernard retired things were going to be different.

"I always thought that when the kids got out of the house, when the time came for Bernard to retire, then *I* was going to retire from housework and would have more time to devote to my catering service." Agnes is a serious cook who, a few years back, started custom-baking fancy desserts for friends and neighbors who appreciated her talent for producing spectacular dishes for special occasions. She is extremely disciplined about her career and works at home on a strict schedule. Despite her hardworking habits her husband, Bernard, expects her to continue with her household duties. Even though she makes money on her catering, Agnes would feel guilty about hiring someone to help her with the cleaning. "If you're working outside the house it's different," she says. "Although my money goes into our joint account, I still must answer to him for every penny I spend."

Bernard has always controlled the money in the family; Agnes was willing to accept this household arrangement because she really likes being married to him and has always gone along with the status quo in order to avoid confrontation. And then something happened to change the picture.

Agnes had an opportunity to invest a modest amount of money with two partners in a small catering and gourmet food shop. Bernard had retired with no financial worries and Agnes felt that he could give her the cash she needed without hardship. She felt she was entitled to a fair share of their retirement money.

During all their years of marriage Agnes had never asked for money for a major purchase. Despite Bernard's financial success she never had a fur coat, jewelry or an extensive wardrobe, and she felt justified in asking him now for money for something she really wanted to do. Her husband not only refused her request, he refused to discuss it.

Agnes was devastated. When she tried to justify her right to share by pointing out how nondemanding she had been in the past and how very important the catering shop was to her, he continued to refuse. Agnes became angry and she mobilized.

She went to the bank to see about a loan. "I was so naive about money," she says. "I realized after I asked the loan officer for money that I had no collateral. I literally own nothing on my own—not my car, not the house. It was a shock."

Agnes went back in defeat to ask Bernard once more to change his mind, but it was no use. And then she did something totally out of character. "I told him I was going to an attorney to see if I had some legal means to force him to give me money." Agnes was not threatening divorce or overt legal action—she just wanted to find out her legal right to money she felt was hers after so many years of marriage. Her husband was stunned. Could this be the sweet, sensitive, docile woman who had always accepted his decisions without question? He relented. He gave her the money and she invested in the shop. Agnes is enthusiastic about her new business, but she feels it would have given her greater pleasure if she did not have to go through so much to get it.

The Volpes' financial problem was not really a problem of finances, but a basic failure to agree on money management and a struggle for power in the family. The Volpes were reduced to emotional blackmail: she, by threatening to consult an outsider to bring legal leverage; he, by remaining inflexible and refusing to recognize her rights as a financial partner in their marriage.

It's not easy to change the marriage pattern of a lifetime, but it can be done. Marriage is a dynamic relationship and is constantly changing. Agnes found this out a little late, but not too late to make an essential change in her marriage.

We're not recommending that you threaten your husband with legal action if he won't let loose of the pursestrings, but if you don't see eye to eye on how your money is handled, turning to a third party might be an excellent idea.

GETTING PROFESSIONAL ADVICE

You might consider going to an investment counselor with your husband. Philip Mullenbach, a registered counselor, insists that both partners in the marriage come for consultation together. "Most women don't know beans about the family finances," says Mullenbach, "but it's never too late for them to start educating themselves. There's something wrong with a retirement picture if the wife does not understand and share control of the family finances." Mullenbach pointed out that the introductory visit to a financial counselor is generally free of charge. Having an objective third party present can make the discussion of money matters with your husband much easier.

Perhaps your income doesn't warrant the services of a private investment counselor (some counselors limit their practice to people who have $200,000 or more to invest). Why don't you and your husband consider going to seminars on finance or taking a course in money management? Should he refuse to go, sign up for the course yourself. Above all, we recommend that you invite your husband to sit down with you and talk about money.

TAKING STOCK

If you have been married forever, if you're still getting the same allowance you got twenty-five years ago, if you charge what you want and then hide in the utility room when the bills arrive on the first of the month, then you must start your financial education. Don't think that because these are lifetime habits, it's too late to learn.

Someone who has always had all the answers is Florence Quinn, who has taken an active part in her family's financial decisions from the day she married Peter Quinn. Now that Peter has retired she continues her involvement in their business affairs. "I do Peter's bookkeeping—he manages some real estate properties from home—I help out with the tax returns and I participate in all decisions concerning our joint investments." Florence smiles. "I even manage a small stock portfolio of my own."

Florence can't understand women who don't insist upon knowing where their money is coming from. "I know some women who are just plain afraid of arithmetic," says Florence. "A woman should do more than just sign the joint tax return—she should read it!" She recommends sending for free government publications on money and retirement; using the library for the numerous sources on budget, estate planning and investment information; and looking into brochures published by the American Association of Retired Persons. Despite Florence's expertise on money matters, she has taken seminars on the subject at her local community center and she recommends them highly.

Florence admits that talking about wills and estates can be a sticky business, and she feels that couples might find it easier to deal with the subject if they take a course in estate planning together.

"I'm appalled at a friend of mine who is afraid to discuss matters of wills and insurance with her husband because he has a history of heart disease," says Florence. "I wouldn't be surprised if she loses as much as a third of her inheritance if he should die before she does."

There are frequent changes in inheritance laws and Florence Quinn is aware of them. Unfortunately, Sandy Morrison is not.

FACING FACTS

Sandy and George Morrison had been married thirty-five years when George retired. "George was the achiever in our marriage. He made all the decisions, and to this day I have no idea of our financial picture," she admits. "George would like me to know what's going on financially, but he's a stinking teacher and I'm a slow learner. I know it's a big mistake not to have a handle on our financial affairs, but I keep pushing it off. George has always excelled at everything he tried, and he has very little patience."

Sandy Morrison's ignorance of their finances is most unfortunate. George Morrison discovered he had cancer six years ago. He decided to retire from his lucrative business as a distributor of automobile accessories and devote the rest of his life to pursuing the interests he had always followed: raising prize flowers, cooking, playing bridge and the stock market and volunteering at the art museum. He shares an interest with his wife, Sandy, in pre-Columbian art. "He's a tough bird," says Sandy with pride. "His attitude is remarkable. He never expresses anxiety; in fact he's inclined to make jokes about serious matters. The other day he said he has had so much radiation he opens all of the garage doors in the neighborhood when he walks down the block." Fortunately George has received an excellent prognosis.

Sandy's failure to share financial responsibility has been the pattern of her married life. Given George's condition, she knows she should face the issue, but she can't. "I wish I had been more assertive when I was younger," says Sandy. A sudden interest in stocks, bonds, wills and inheritance taxes does not seem appropriate to her at this time.

Statistics show that you and your husband have every right to look forward to years of a healthy and happy retirement. Even with the gift of those years, the odds are that you will have to face your final years alone. Actuarial tables illustrate that most women survive their husbands. What you don't know about your estate *can* hurt you.

Don't be afraid to ask questions about your finances. Here are but a few of the things you must have answers to if you are going to face retirement with a degree of equanimity about money:

- What is the present value of your home?
- How much is your automobile worth?
- What is your joint annual income from real estate, pensions, stocks, bonds, Social Security and investments?
- Do you own stocks and bonds jointly?
- Do you each own securities separately?
- How much life insurance does your husband carry?

- Are you the beneficiary?
- Do you have a joint bank account?
- Do you have separate bank accounts?
- Do you have an up-to-date will?
- Do you rent a safe-deposit box?
- Do you know where the key is?

You might be pleasantly surprised to find that you really have more than you thought—that your accumulation of stocks, the value of your house and car, pension funds and other income sources add up to more than you expected.

MONEY TALKS

Perhaps talking about money has always been difficult for you, or maybe it is a charged subject as far as your husband is concerned. More than in-laws, more than children, more than sex, the subject of money is a major source of friction in most marriages. Your approach to money matters will determine the I.Q. (irritation quotient) the handling of money in your family produces. Can you agree on spending priorities? At what point does a project or a purchase become unaffordable? Do you have a realistic grasp of your financial situation to help you make a convincing argument for something you really want, or really want to do?

The subject can be addressed without major hostilities ensuing. Believe us. Let's look at what might be a typical dialogue between husband and wife about money.

Meet Betty. She's not sure what her financial setup is because her husband Bob handles the checkbook. Betty would love to get away from home for a few days just for a change of scenery, and a trip to New York is her idea of fun and excitement. She approaches her husband, Bob, like a little girl asking her daddy for a lollipop.

BETTY: Bob, honey, let's take a long weekend in

New York. Wouldn't you love to see a Broadway play and go to some good restaurants?

BOB: Are you kidding! Do you know how expensive New York is?

BETTY: Oh, but it would be so much fun to go there for a few days.

BOB: We can't afford it, so forget about it.

BETTY: (whining) Why don't we ever have enough money to spend on what I want? You always have money to spend on what you want.

BOB: Like what?

BETTY: Like the new lawn mower...

If Betty knew her financial situation this conversation would have taken quite a different turn. In fact, her awareness might give her an insight into her husband's true feeling about a trip to New York.

BETTY: Bob, honey, let's take a long weekend in New York. Wouldn't you love to see a Broadway play and go to some good restaurants?

BOB: Are you kidding! Do you know how expensive New York is?

BETTY: I can shop around for an inexpensive air fare and we can stay at a hotel on a weekend rate.

BOB: It's still too much money.

BETTY: I looked over our budget for this month and I know we can afford it. Be honest. Would you rather not go to New York?

BOB: To tell you the truth, I don't like New York.

BETTY: You should have said so. What about New Orleans?

BOB: Great. We could have dinner at Antoine's.

BETTY: It's too expensive!

The smarter you are about your budget, the less likely it is that your husband will use money as a subterfuge. Of course, the ideal conversation would go as follows:

BETTY: Bob, honey, let's take a long weekend in New York. Wouldn't you love to see a Broadway play and go to some good restaurants?

BOB: I would like to get away, but I'm not that excited about going to New York. I really would like to go to New Orleans; do you think our budget could take it?

BETTY: I've gone over the checkbook and I know it can. And you're on for New Orleans.

BOB: Great! We'll go to New York next time.

What makes this last dialogue an ideal exchange is that Betty is well aware of their financial situation, and Bob is honest about what he wants to do. No subterfuge here.

WHEN RETIREMENT MEANS RETRENCHMENT

You and your husband have communicated. You have made plans for his retirement and you both know that with some cutting back you'll be able to live comfortably on that income. Because you do not want to invade your capital, you realize that there is going to have to be a degree of retrenchment. You are not going to be as free with money as you had been without the monthly income and yearly bonuses coming in.

So it's no more expensive French restaurants, no more designer shoes, fewer nights at the theater, and more meat loaf. Can you adjust to the change?

Penny and Earl Engle did, and in a most intelligent way. Earl Engle found himself retired at the relatively young age of 53 when his real estate business declined during a business recession. Rather than try to hold on, Earl decided that with careful planning he could close the doors to his office, avoid the grief of seeing his business fail and retire on a reasonable income.

"Earl did look for other jobs," says Penny, "and he

attended seminars with an eye to reentering business, but there wasn't anything lucrative enough available for him to put in those hours." Earl had worked on Saturdays and Sundays for all of their married life as well as working nights, and now they were able to have the time together that they had never had before. "It's wonderful," says Penny. "Now we're just like everyone else. We even go out for brunch together on Sundays."

Because theirs was a premature retirement, the Engles realized that they would have to be extremely careful with their investments and with their spending. They are young and active people, and they have many years ahead of them. The last thing they intend to do is dig into their capital, and they are both involved in trying to make their net worth appreciate. Retrenchment for them meant some basic changes in their way of life.

"We have always been rather conservative about our spending," says Penny, "so it wasn't too great an adjustment. We feel that we live very nicely even if we don't spend as much as some of our friends do on travel and dining out."

There are several reasons why Penny has made the adjustment successfully. First and foremost, she knows what their financial situation is. She discusses all decisions about money with Earl, and even though she doesn't take the active part in making investments that Florence Quinn does, Penny knows what's going on. Knowing where you stand can dispel an unreasonable fear of the unknown.

The second reason Penny does not feel deprived is a very personal one. Penny recently lost her mother. Before her death Penny's mother lived with the Engles for four years. Her mother was a stroke victim and Penny undertook her complete care. Earl not only accepted his mother-in-law's presence in his home, he pitched in in a way that was most unusual. "Earl would stay with Mom so I could go out to play tennis or take an exercise class," says Penny. "In fact, one morning I left before my mother awoke. When I returned I found

that Earl not only got her up and had made her breakfast, he was brushing her hair. I nearly wept."

Since her mother's death, Penny and Earl have joined
a "caring committee" associated with their church. They
started out by visiting the elderly in a nursing home
one day a week. "We just talk to the residents, hold
their hands, and listen to what they have to say. The
first time we went it was very emotional, but now it
is much easier and we get great satisfaction from it."
Their volunteer work is extremely important to them
and fills a need that others might fill with extravagant
spending.

The third reason that Penny has made an excellent
adjustment to cutting back on her standard of living
is that she is by nature an initiator. Before Earl's retirement she was the one among their circle of friends
who found the new and interesting restaurant, the art
fair, the lecture, the unusual movie or play. And she
still does. Penny insists that she has found excellent
restaurants that are very inexpensive. "I can't see
spending $60 for just the two of us for dinner," she says.
Penny plans trips that they take by car that are interesting. They returned from nine days in Toronto,
stayed home for a week and then drove to Michigan to
visit the wineries! They stay at modestly priced places
and they love it. They support community theater productions and avoid going to expensive plays in the city.

The Engles lead a more interesting and exciting life
on less money than many people who have much more
to spend.

THEY CUT BACK, TOO

Cutting back for Doris and Alfred Harris would be
living it up for the Engles. Though their retirement
income is generous compared to that of the Engles',
Doris insists, "We're definitely more conservative in
our spending and think twice before we plan a trip."

Alfred Harris sold his seat on the Commodities Exchange after a series of shrewd speculations in soybean futures that have ensured him financial security for the rest of the Harrises' lives. Alfred had always dreamed of being an architect, so at age 55 he returned to school, studied hard, completed the course, got his license and subsequently designed a two-family condominium which he put up for sale. The project cost more than the Harrises had anticipated, and even after the condos were sold they suffered some financial loss. Doris says, "We're still more secure than we were before when Al was in a high-risk, high-income business he didn't enjoy and over which he had no control. We've reexamined our priorities and made choices. It's never fun to retrench; we gave up some luxuries we used to take for granted, like dining out almost every night, and we're much more careful with our spending in general than we were. We still do most everything we want; we're just more selective."

BE AN EARLY BIRD

If you arrive at some restaurants a little earlier than the traditional dinner hour, chances are you qualify as an early bird.

Early birds can order a full dinner at 5 p.m. for half the price of the very same meal served at 7 p.m., and this takes place in some of the nicest restaurants in town.

Martha and Tom Warren have made a game of being early birds. The Warrens live in Florida, where they appreciate the lower cost of living. Martha is a walking testimonial to the art of making the most of available bargains. She scans the newspapers looking for new restaurants, particularly those that feature early-bird dinners, and in their home town of Fort Lauderdale the range of dining bargains is almost limitless. "One of our favorites is a seafood restaurant that features a

two-for-one lobster dinner," says Martha. "We each order a full dinner, share one and take the leftovers home
for lobster salad the next day."

Everyone takes home doggie bags in the community
where they live. In fact, it's expected. Portions in many
restaurants are unusually generous and restaurants
have carry-out containers ready to go.

Taking home leftovers is accepted protocol in many
areas with large retirement populations. When Lila
and Herb Wallace had dinner with friends recently,
they were asked by the waitress if they wanted to take
home their untouched loaf of French bread. Lila declined graciously. When they left the restaurant and
went to their car, they heard someone calling out, "Hey,
Missus, wait..." They turned to see a busboy sprinting
toward them in the parking lot. "You forgot your bread,"
he panted, and thrust the package of French bread at
Lila. She accepted it with thanks and then drove around
with the package in her car for the next three days!

QUIRKY ECONOMIES

When your husband's regular paycheck stops—beware! You may find yourself behaving strangely. You
know, saving odd bits of string and washing and drying
paper plates. Worse yet, your husband might be bitten
by the economy bug and insist upon driving around
the block fifty times until he finds a parking meter
that hasn't expired.

Of course, using discount coupons, watching for su-
permarket sales, seeking less expensive entertain-
ments are practices to be recommended and admired,
but if either one of you becomes obsessive about your
coups with coupons or funky finds from the flea market,
you may be faced with a common retirement syndrome:
a case of quirky economies.

Helen Hamilton's husband, Matt, has taken over the
grocery shopping since he retired as manager of a chain
of parking lots. It's a boon to Helen, who had just about

run out of menu ideas. Under the new management, groceries are purchased only on Thursdays because Thursday is double coupon day. Wonderful—but not so wonderful if Helen runs out of bread, milk or cheese on Monday. Matt won't let her go near a grocery store until Thursday. She's taken to sneaking Kellogg's All Bran home like an alcoholic who tries to hide a bottle of Wild Turkey.

Betsy Dawes's husband Ed gets positively ecstatic every time he finds a coupon for Fleischmann's margarine. He also covets those coupons for Charmin toilet tissue and Lipton's lemon-flavored, Nutra-Sweetened iced tea mix. The result is that Betsy has a freezer filled to the top with margarine but has been out of mayonnaise for three weeks, because Ed is confident that his favorite brand will be couponed soon and then, if he buys it on double coupon day—well, that's as good as a hole-in-one. In the meantime, they're swallowing their BLTs dry.

Then there's John Goodspeed, who told his wife, Ellen, that now that he was retired they would realize immediate savings in the maintenance of their home. She was to dismiss the gardening service, forget about hiring a painter for the outside trim and cancel the plasterer because *he* was going to repair the spots where the plaster had cracked. That was five years ago. When Ellen reminds him of his good intentions he says, "Not now, dear—I'm reading the paper."

"When John worked the house was in much better repair and I haven't noticed the savings he talked about," says Ellen.

Sara Leland's husband, Frank, will drive ten miles to buy vitamins which are 20 percent less than those at the corner drugstore. "Frank has become neurotic about money since he retired," says Sara. "He doesn't want to know what we have. I give him his allowance, which puts a lot of pressure on me to make ends meet. I don't think Frank would mind if I bought myself a mink coat, but he'll argue with me for not buying a generic brand of pickles. He thinks he's 'saving' by going to garage sales and auctions every day and we've ended up with a houseful of junk. Then if we run short of money it's my fault."

You'll be able to tell when your compulsive economies are false economies or, to put it more succinctly, when you become downright cheap, by your friends' reactions.

HOW TO LOSE FRIENDS

Lila and Herb Wallace (you remember, she drove around with the bread in her car) no longer enjoy dining out with their oldest and dearest friends, the Chases, since Sam Chase retired. "I don't mind scaling down in our choice of restaurants," says Lila, "but I hate it when Sam won't let his wife order anything on the menu without his supervision. He'll either say, 'You can't have the cole slaw, it's extra' or 'You'll have to have the dessert, it's included.'" Lila says it's so embarrassing to see Sam cheat on the tip or fumble in coming up with his share of the bill that frequently Herb Wallace pays the tab altogether.

SUMMING IT UP

How you manage your retirement funds is really up to the two of you. To keep the subject friction-free you would do well to do the following:
- Be sure you know the reality of your financial situation.
- Know the sources of your income and the amount of capital that you have.
- Take an active part in making investment and spending decisions.
- Be completely aware of the amount of insurance you have and the provisions of your wills.
- Go to professionals: a qualified insurance broker, an attorney, a registered investment counselor—

or attend courses or seminars that will expand your knowledge of financial matters.

- Learn to cut back without cutting out those things you enjoy doing.
- Question some of your economies. Do you really save money or are they false economies?
- Communicate! Talk to your husband about your finances without rancor. If the lines of communication are open there will be less cause for trouble.
- Keep on clipping those sale coupons—but *only* for products you will really use.

7
MAKING THE BIG MOVE

*I don't miss the sound of kids
making noise and if I really
have a yen to see youngsters
there are plenty of them in
the supermarkets.*
Maureen Piercy

Pearl Richman gave her husband a surprise retirement/birthday party last September 18. John Richman was 65 on that day. He retired from his law practice on September 26, and on September 27 the Richmans packed up their car and headed for Rancho Sante Fe, California, and their new retirement home.

The Richmans had never lived in California; they are from the Midwest. They had never been in Rancho Santa Fe except for the two weeks they stayed there when they bought their new home. They knew absolutely no one except the real estate agent who sold them the property and the plumber who put in their hot tub.

The Richmans are not unusual. Retirement often signals a time when couples consider a major move. For some it's a move from the heavy winters up north to the warm climate of the Sun Belt states. For others it's a move from a large suburban home to a compact city apartment. There are numerous reasons why people who retire often move and money is a major one.

A MATTER OF MONEY

"There are two sure things you can bet on," Joe Pick would tell his wife, Thelma. "One is that I'll never retire and the other is that I'll never live in Florida." But Joe Pick was mistaken. He found himself odd man out when the New York advertising agency for which he worked merged with a large public relations firm. He was a reluctant retiree at age 63.

Thelma and Joe Pick always lived in New York and it was there that they hoped to spend their retirement years. During the first year of Joe's retirement the Picks continued to maintain their Upper West Side apartment and tried to make a go of it living in New York. While he was working, Joe made an excellent salary but had not managed to parlay his savings into an income that would keep pace with inflation. "We became very money conscious," says Thelma. "Living in New York is so expensive; an evening out was prohibitive. I made do with my existing wardrobe and I even stopped entertaining at home. It costs a lot of money to throw a nice party and rather than do something halfway I did nothing at all." Thelma looks embarrassed. "I stopped accepting invitations because I didn't want to be put in the position of having to reciprocate. Joe and I began to question the value of having to live so penuriously just to meet our mortgage payments."

It took about two years after Joe left the agency for them to decide to sell their apartment, invest the proceeds and buy a comfortable two-bedroom town house in Pompano Beach, Florida. "We have friends who live in Pompano Beach, and we knew we would be able to live graciously on a lot less money than we were spending in New York City.

"I looked forward to starting over, going to a new home in a warm climate," says Thelma. "I thought life would be more carefree. Do you know we have a forty-year mortgage?" Thelma laughs. "When we signed the final papers on the house the developer asked us to choose the carpeting we preferred. For the first time in my life I realized I didn't care if the carpeting wasn't the best grade."

The Picks had solved their money problems, but they didn't live happily ever after.

A MATTER OF ADJUSTMENT

Thelma and Joe Pick selected the few pieces of furniture they wanted to keep and set off for their new home in Florida with mixed emotions: Thelma, with excited anticipation; Joe, with trepidation.

Not even the dog made a good adjustment.

Joe, who said he would never retire and would never live in Florida, found the move much more difficult than Thelma did. He missed the fast pace of New York City, but it was being forced out of his job in advertising that had the most devastating effect on him—more than either Thelma or he realized. "Joe took his angst out on me," complains Thelma. "Nothing I did was right. He gave me the silent treatment and that's worse than an all-out argument."

The Picks weren't in Florida more than four months when Joe asked Thelma to go back to New York with him for a visit. But the lines of communication had broken down. "He had been so negative," says Thelma. "I didn't want to give in to him." She decided to stay put in Pompano Beach and told him he could go himself if that was what he wanted. And that's just what Joe did.

Thelma felt no relief when Joe left. She found herself stewing about their situation. "There seemed to be no answer to our problem. After thirty-nine years together I was miserable when he was here and I was miserable when he was gone." At the end of the week Joe called from New York. Thelma was defensive until she heard him say, "Please bear with me until I get over this hump." When he returned to Florida, Joe was able to sit down and talk with Thelma. She realized just how devastating the retirement had been for him, and Joe admitted he had done little to help himself.

Things have improved for the Picks. Joe volunteers his services doing public relations work for the local hospital and Thelma is back in the social swing. "There are still some rough days," says Thelma, "but we're adjusting to our life here. The important thing is that we feel we have a future together."

The Picks considered their move for two years before going to Florida. As much as they were prepared intellectually for this change in their lives, they were not prepared for the emotional adjustment the move would demand. A more successful adjustment to an unexpected move was made by Della and Harry Nagle, who were faced with what seemed to them to be an overnight decision on Harry's retirement.

Harry, an oral surgeon, was only 54 years old when he discovered he was losing his sight. He was finally forced to retire. "It was really a shock," says Della. "We still had one son in college and another in graduate school, and, although we lived conservatively, we knew that we had to make some drastic changes in our way of life if we were going to make it financially." Like the Picks, the Nagles sold their home and invested the proceeds for future income, but unlike the Picks, they did not move away to another state.

For twenty-five years Della and Harry Nagle had lived in a large suburban home in Olympia Fields, Illinois. Harry was an avid gardener and Della was active in local politics. It was a wrench when the Nagles sold their house and moved to a one-bedroom high-rise apartment on the north side of Chicago. "I miss the house," Della says. "Although we have a very pleasant apartment in a large, well-managed building, it's impersonal. I don't know any of my neighbors—I was friendly with *everyone* on the block where we used to live." With this potentially difficult living situation, the Nagles succeeded more quickly in adjusting to their retirement than did the Picks. Why? For several reasons.

To begin with, Della and Harry talk to each other. She is very empathetic and understands how crushing his eyesight loss is. He, in turn, is aware of the sacrifices she has been willing to make in order to relieve their financial burden.

Della was creative and arranged their small apartment so that they both have their own space. She turned the dining alcove into a den where Harry can enjoy television and put her own desk in the master bedroom.

Although the Nagles left Olympia Fields, they still live in the Chicago area and thus are able to continue seeing old friends.

A most important point: Harry Nagle has retained his identity as a well-known oral surgeon in Chicago. He continues as a consultant. Unlike Joe Pick, he does not have to reestablish his reputation. When a man retires, his prestige remains stable when he stays in his same milieu. When you stay where you are known, it is easier to adopt new interests and new activities.

Harry Nagle's experience bears out this point. And although Della gave up the close day-to-day involvement with neighbors and community activities that she had enjoyed in the suburbs, she traded them for a long list of city-based activities: she joined a book club and a baroque music group and even became a docent with an architecture society, conducting tours of Chicago's famous Loop. "I still see some of my old friends. But friends are a matter of geographic convenience," says Della. "Your intellectual curiosity is like a religion— you take it with you wherever you go, and if you can share it with someone you love and admire nothing can rob you of that joy."

Both the Picks and the Nagles had retirement thrust upon them, and both were pained by having to move from their homes of many years to new surroundings. The Nagles were supportive of each other and wanted the move to work. They shared the disappointment of Harry's abbreviated career and their reduced circumstances and together made every effort to adapt. They had the continuing support of old friendships, and Dr. Nagle was still recognized by the professional community for his accomplishments. Joe Pick not only lost his job, he lost his identity. Back in New York he was known as a top advertising man; in Pompano Beach, Florida, he was unknown. He felt isolated and was not ready to make new friends. Thelma, who was more than ready to settle into her new retirement life in Florida, lost patience with Joe when he was unable to adjust. Although they had both agreed to the move, the move didn't agree with them.

TAKE YOUR TIME

No matter what the circumstances of your husband's retirement, don't make any hasty moves. Take your time about making that decision to locate in a new community. Once you do your homework you should find the right place to live, and then the change can be exciting. At a time when life can be humdrum, when you and your husband have run out of things to say to each other, a move to a new home, a new community, a new climate can refuel your relationship.

RETIREMENT COMMUNITIES
FUN IN THE SUN

Jane Ruggles testifies to the fact that a move can be stimulating to a relationship. The Ruggles had vacationed in the Palm Springs area for several winters and knew that it was where they would eventually settle. "We picked out the condo we wanted the year before Bill retired," says Jane. "It was smaller than our house in Pittsburgh, but it was sunny and cheerful and we couldn't wait to live in it."

Jane's husband, Bill, was the senior partner of a large Pittsburgh law firm. He retired by choice and

was royally feted at a testimonial dinner attended by
friends, clients and fellow lawyers. It was with a sense
of accomplishment and completion that he headed for
their retirement home in California.

"It was so different from when we moved into our
first home," Jane continues. "I made all of the fur-
nishing decisions then because Bill was occupied with
his business career. This time Bill became involved in
every choice for the house. He even helped pick out the
kitchen towels. We really enjoyed ourselves. We drove
to Los Angeles, stayed in a hotel and went shopping
for carpeting, draperies and furniture. Then after
everything was delivered and the house came together,
we stood back and admired our excellent taste."

Jane laughs. "It's a little like being newly married.
We are more intimate than ever. Sometimes I think
we're playing house. We really haven't had any adjustment problems," she says. "We miss our friends and
family back home, but the payoff is that we've become
closer to each other."

There's good reason for the Ruggles' successful retirement. Bill Ruggles had no regrets about leaving his
work. He and Jane had time to plan their retirement.
They had tested Palm Springs and knew that they liked
it. Income from investments and retirement funds made
it possible for Bill and Jane to retire without financial
stress. They had everything going for them.

Other retirees bloomed in the sun, too. Scottsdale,
Tucson and Phoenix received high marks from women
we talked to who had rerooted in Arizona.

"Most of our neighbors are retired and we like it that
way," says Maureen Piercy. Maureen and Sal Piercy
enjoy the easy living of Scottsdale and its proximity to
Phoenix. "Phoenix is the ninth-largest city in the United
States," she boasts. The Piercys live in an adult complex with swimming pools, tennis courts and covenants
restricting families with children under 18. "I don't
miss the sound of kids making noise, and, if I really
have the yen to see youngsters, there are plenty of them
in the supermarkets," says Maureen. "Life here is much

slower-paced, more relaxing, and not for a minute do we long for the Chicago winters."

The Ruggles and the Piercys enjoy their lives in communities that attract retirees, but not everyone in their housing development is retired. However, there are communities planned for retired people exclusively.

LIFE IN THE SLOW LANE

"Everything you need for a fresh beginning and a quality retirement."

"Enjoy life in the sun. Retire to your own custom-built home and lot for $29,900."

"Retire to sun-kissed Florida for only $25,995."

"Eleven different floor plans in Retirement Village from $60,000 to $162,000."

All this and (depending on the adult community you choose) free golf, security police, cable TV, outdoor barbecue, fishing, swimming, arts and crafts, Jacuzzi, patios, tennis, shuffleboard, exclusive country club atmosphere, lavish guarded entrance to ensure privacy and security.

If you've ever read the real estate ads you've seen these descriptions of planned communities where every blade of grass is in its appointed place. Or perhaps in your travels you've visited El Dorado, Happy Horizons, Rancho Riviera, The Lakes, The Palms, or any one of the thousands of planned retirement villages in the United States.

Celia and Jerry Landers were on their way to a business convention in San Francisco when they made a detour to visit their niece who had just bought a condominium in Arizona. They knew immediately that this was the place for them, put a down payment on a house not yet under construction, and three years later when Jerry retired they called the movers and were off to spend the rest of their lives in Sun City West, Arizona.

Sun City West is a structured Arizona retirement community. Celia's sister May, who visits her each year, describes life in Sun City West as "sterile," but Celia says it's paradise for retirees who don't want to work too hard thinking up ways to keep happily busy. She uses words like "great," "fabulous" and "spectacular" to describe the activities center, the exercise facilities, the golf courses (spectacular); the shuffleboard, the walking and running paths, the square dancing and outdoor concerts (fabulous); not to mention the silver and gold jewelry-making classes, which are "great."

"It's easy living and it's inexpensive," she says. The Landers moved into a three-bedroom, two-bath house in Sun City West for under $30,000 some years ago. Celia claims today's housing prices in Sun City West are still low when compared with housing elsewhere in the country.

She continues: "There are no schools, so taxes are low. Sun City West is unincorporated and we spend a lot of money to keep it that way. We don't have a municipal government or a police department to underwrite; we do have a sheriff's posse and many neighbors serve as volunteers to keep Sun City West the way it is. Almost everyone I know gets involved in town meetings.

"There are really two communities," Celia points out, "Sun City and Sun City West. The younger people (those in their fifties and sixties) settle in Sun City West and are considered the swinging younger group. It depends on what you're looking for in retirement. Jerry and I are from a small town in North Dakota and we're happy with the small-town neighborly feeling in Sun City West. We like being with people of our own generation; our children are so scattered geographically, it doesn't matter where we live. There's an enormous medical setup and doctors flock to Sun City West because they love the facilities. But some people settle here, and then leave after a year or two because they cannot adjust to being with people who are all the same age."

A University of Michigan study of retirement communities revealed that there are close to 3,000 adult community developments in the United States, most of them clustered in the sun-drenched states of Florida, California and Arizona. There are a growing number of adult communities in northern states as well which offer similar options to retirees. You don't have to follow the sun to find retirement communities; they are sprinkled throughout every region of the United States, and with a little sleuthing you can undoubtedly find several to investigate in your own area.

SHANGRI-LA NORTH

Vivian and Douglas Raney heard of Leisure Village in Fox Lake, Illinois, through ads on radio and television. They had friends who lived in a leisure community in California, "but there was nothing to pull us there," says Vivian. "We wanted to stay in this area."

Until their retirement the Raneys had lived in a large home on several acres in Deerfield, Illinois. Doug Raney was a schoolteacher and during the summer months he and Vivian operated a successful summer camp in their spacious house.

"I worked with Doug all the years we ran the camp," says patrician, white-haired Vivian Raney. "I was in charge of the finances for the camp and for our family. I worked with young campers and I raised our own three children as well. It's not hard to understand why an all-adult community appealed to me when Doug retired from his teaching job. I had some passing regrets when we sold the house and the camp. It would have been a nice place for our children to bring their families, but it was the lawn that did us in!"

Vivian and Doug liked the idea of living in a pleasant community where the maintenance of lawns and walks are someone else's responsibility. After a lifetime of working with youngsters, the prospect of quiet days guaranteed to be free of noisy neighborhood children sounded better all the time. "We didn't spend a lot of time making up our minds about Leisure Village," says Vivian. "Once we decide we want something we go after it. I like to do things spontaneously. Sometimes Doug holds me back but mostly he goes along with me."

Leisure Village has worked out well for the Raneys. Vivian runs a monthly book review group. Both she and Doug play golf and they are able to drive into town whenever they need groceries or want to go out for an evening's entertainment. They have made many casual and a few close friendships among their neighbors. "Our block is the best," says Vivian proudly, "and we have the best block party in the village."

Things have changed since the Raneys first moved to Leisure Village in 1978. As pioneers in the housing project, they enjoyed the early period when the developers were luring prospective buyers with a wide range of amenities. "Everything was lush, lush, lush then," says Vivian. "We had daily shuttle bus service to town. There was a regular activities newsletter and the maintenance service couldn't be beat. There were supposed to be 1,500 houses built here, which would mean very low assessments for each of us for maintenance of the pool, golf course and other extras the village offers. The final development turned out to be only 300 houses." Vivian continues: "The developers have pulled out, the condominium association has taken over, services have decreased and the costs have escalated. But if we had to do it over, after weighing the pros and cons, I believe we'd do the same thing."

A look at the Leisure Village activities calendar for one week in July shows that there's not a lot of leisure at Leisure Village:

Monday	8:30 a.m.	Poker in Billiard Room
	10:00 a.m.	Summer Bowl at Johnsburg
	1:00 p.m.	Quilting in Sewing Room
	1:00 p.m.	Bridge in Lounge B
	4:30–5:15 p.m.	Water Exercise Class
	6:30 p.m.	8-Ball Pool Tournament
Tuesday	10:30 a.m.	Women's Golf League
	10:30 a.m.	Shopping at Randhurst
	10:30 a.m.	Arlington Park Race Track
	1:00 p.m.	Poker in Billiard Room
	1:30 p.m.	Investment Club
	7:00 p.m.	Bingo in Auditorium
Wednesday	10–noon	Men's Golf League
	1:00 p.m.	Gin Rummy in Lounge B
	1–3 p.m.	Trick Painting
	2–4 p.m.	Crafts in Sewing Room
	7:00 p.m.	AARP Meeting
Thursday	8:30 a.m.	Poker in Billiard Room

	10:45 a.m.	Tap Class in Auditorium
	11:00 a.m.	Cubs Ballgame
	1:00 p.m.	Shopping—Antioch
	2:00 p.m.	Blood Pressure
	5:00 p.m.	Richards Picnic (seven tables)
	7:00 p.m.	Maintenance Meeting
Friday	8:30 a.m.	Poker in Billiard Room
	10:00 a.m.	Water Exercise
	10:00 a.m.	Finance Meeting
	10:45 a.m.	Budget Work Session
	1:00 p.m.	Shopping— McHenry
	2:00 p.m.	Bingo in Auditorium
	5:00 p.m.	Fish Boil
	7:00 p.m.	Ballroom Dancing
	7:30 p.m.	Kitchen Band Practice
Saturday	8:30 a.m.	Poker in Billiard Room
	10:00 a.m.	Bridge in Lounge B
	12:30 p.m.	Shopping— Randhurst
	4:30 p.m.	Leonard Picnic
	4:30 p.m.	Halstead Picnic
	4:30 p.m.	Powers Picnic (Rain: Lounge B)
Sunday	7:00 p.m.	Bingo

FIRST THE GOOD NEWS

There's good news and bad news about living in the structured environment of an adult community.

- You need never be bored. There are meetings, block parties, special interest groups (card games, investment groups, book review groups, Bingo games)—an activities list long enough and diverse enough to appeal to almost everyone's taste and interest.

- Most adult communities offer country club living with golf, swimming, tennis, shuffleboard and other exercise facilities.

- One of the basic perks of adult community living is maintenance of manicured lawns and carefree landscaping.

- Residents of adult communities frequently pay very low taxes because there are few, if any, school-age children to educate.

- Adult communities are just that—for adults. If you can do without the noise of children shouting and splashing in your pool while you're trying to swim laps, it might be just the place for you. In many adult communities families with children under the age of 18 are not eligible to buy.

- Neighbors often become part of a network of friends who provide help and security for each other.

- Many adult communities have security entrance gates.

The bad news

- If you purchase your house while the development is still in the selling stage, you may be surprised at the increase of assessments after the developer leaves and the residents take over management.
- Shopping centers are not always near adult community developments. If you don't drive, you might feel isolated from shopping, movies and restaurants.
- "No children" means *your* grandchildren as well as everyone else's. While youngsters can visit, they cannot move in with grandma and grandpa. A notice posted for residents of one adult community we visited warned: "Because this is an adult community precautions have *not* been taken to childproof the facilities. Children should not be allowed to wander around the village without an adult present."
- In a controlled environment individualizing the appearance of your own house and lot is frowned upon; changes in basic architectural design are prohibited.

*M*AKING FRIENDS

A word of caution: When you settle into your new retirement home and the doorbell rings—and believe us, it will ring—be prepared to greet a friendly neighbor who will present you with a cake, or flowers, or even a bottle of wine. Don't throw your arms around her neck and dampen her cheek with your tears no matter how lonely you are. Be pleasant. Be gracious. Beware. She may be the needy one and you'll spend the next six months trying to get her out of your kitchen.

We know this is cynical and even a slight overstatement, but we assure you, *you will make friends*. Just take your time doing it.

Don't count on your husband to make your social contacts. Men are usually reticent in this area. We women are by nature friend makers, and you'll probably be the one to break the social ice.

Laura and Ted Pierce are a good example. They both play tennis, and when they moved to their new house in Carmel, California, Ted was the first one to find a daily tennis game.

Several weeks later Laura teamed up with Marcia Bigelow for a morning game of singles. Within three days Laura knew that Marcia was originally from Massachusetts, that her husband was a retired surgeon, that she had three children and that she recently had had a hysterectomy. On the fourth day Laura invited the Bigelows over for drinks and an informal barbecue. It was only when Marcia and Will Bigelow arrived at the Pierces that Ted announced that Will Bigelow was the man he had been playing doubles with each morning for six weeks.

"Ted only knew him as Will," says Laura. "All he told me was that he had a great backhand!" The Bigelows and the Pierces now have dinner together often.

Here are some of the places you will make friends:
- On the tennis court
- On the golf course
- At the country club
- At church
- At your volunteer job
- At classes you take
- At community club meetings
- At the senior center

And, of course, don't forget your neighbors. They can be terrific.

BEFORE THE BIG MOVE

If you and your husband are ready for a change and think a move to a new home might be just the thing, we advise that you first do the following:

• *Talk to each other.* Find out if you each have the same thing in mind. Does he want to move to the city? Do you prefer to live in the suburbs? Be honest about your real feelings. Don't say you'd love a small apartment in the city just to please him. (The workbook quiz in Chapter 11 should help you communicate on this subject.)

• *Do some hard research.* Read up on the area that you wish to move to. Is the climate right? Is it near shops, theaters, churches, medical centers, and those facilities you need to make life comfortable?

• *Talk to people who have made a similar move.* Ask them to be honest about the pros and cons. For example, if you are contemplating a move to the city from the suburbs, talk to someone who has made the same move. Find out if she thinks the stimulation of city life makes up for urban noise and congestion.

• *Be prepared to compromise.* He wants to unload the large suburban house because its maintenance is getting him down. You dread the thought of high-rise apartment living. Why not list the possible alternatives? Consider a no-care suburban condominium or rental apartment. Many apartment and townhouse developments, both rental and condo, have sprung up in the suburbs because of the growing demand for these units by a maturing population.

• *Take a trial run.* If you both think a move to the South or West would be just the thing, why not rent a home for a season to see if you both like it?

ADVICE FROM AARP

Here are some additional things you'll need to consider before making your final decision to make the Big Move, according to the American Association of Retired Persons (AARP). Your new housing and locale should come as close as possible to satisfying these basic needs:
- Health—a climate and housing suited to your physical condition
- Economic security—an amount you can afford for your way of life
- Status—a position or voice in the community
- Friendship—a place where you already have friends or an opportunity to make them

REMEMBER THE RICHMANS?

They moved to their new home in Rancho Santa Fe, California, when we introduced you to them at the beginning of this chapter. We spoke to Pearl Richman on the telephone, and she sounded a little at sea. "The house is nearly in order," says Pearl. "My daughter and son-in-law came down from Oregon to give us a hand and we're grateful.

"John is going out to look for a boat. It has been the dream of his life to own his own fishing boat and now is the time.

"I seem to have developed an allergy, but maybe it's just nerves. My next-door neighbor came over and I like her, but I'm taking your advice and I'm going slow. We're going to give Rancho Santa Fe our best shot." Pearl paused. "If we don't like it, we can always move."

8
STAYING
HEALTHY

Just when gravity has made
my skin collapse, my hus-
band's eyes have aged and he
doesn't see a line in my face!
Marilyn Biondi

The best thing for you and your husband's health
during the retirement years is to keep active and
to keep interested.

A little too much leisure and you start to feel every
ache and pain. A lot of leisure and the aches and pains
become the focus of your life and, even worse, the topic
of your conversation. Think a minute. How often have
you found yourself trapped with someone who wanted
to tell you about her hiatal hernia or incipient gall-
bladder disease?

Ellen Goodspeed recalls a party she and her husband
attended given by a high-level State Department of-
ficial for an international assembly of guests. She was
thrilled when she found her dinner partner was a man
who had been a close associate of Dag Hammarskjöld
and had been to the South Pole. "Do you know what
he talked about all evening?" asked Ellen. "His excess
of uric acid!"

Don't let yourself think that retirement means a
future of failing health and chronic illness. "Sickness

is one thing, aging is quite another," says *Retirement Living* magazine. "They don't have to go together and most often, they don't.

"Heart attacks among men between the ages of 34 and 65 were found to be 50 percent higher than among men *over* 65, and arthritis hits hardest in the age group 25 to 40. Of all cancer deaths, 44 percent are among persons *under* 65. On the other hand, people who live to 75 have a capacity to resist viruses and bacteria." The article goes on to state that of the millions of Americans 65 or older, at least 96 out of every 100 are in reasonably good health.

The important point is that now that your husband is retired you want him to stay healthy and you want to stay that way yourself.

YOU ARE WHAT YOU EAT

Unless you've been hiding under a rock, you know all about the relationship between nutrition and health— the effect of what you eat on your general well-being. By this time, one or the other of you has been advised to watch your diet: to combat cholesterol (high); blood pressure (high or low); diabetes (latent or galloping). If you've reached retirement age you undoubtedly know that eggs, dairy products and saturated fats raise cholesterol levels and that sodium is a major contributor to hypertension. And as for sugar, we all know what sugar can do. It's not only fattening, it can alter our moods so that we feel we're on an emotional roller coaster.

If we're so smart, why is it that so many of us still have trouble keeping that weight off, or the blood pressure down, or forming habits that will help us enjoy our retirement years to the fullest?

These are not easy questions to answer, but with your husband retired it would seem a perfect opportunity to shape up. After all, you have time to pay attention to the ways you eat and exercise, and you can work on improving your health habits together. Now that he's retired, things are going to be different. *Both* of you are going to go on a nutritionally sound eating program. Since he has also retired from the three-martini business lunch, the two of you can turn your attention to the business of sound nutritional management. You will plan your meals together, take turns cooking, and grocery shopping will be a family affair.

But wait a minute; there's a minor problem: he has no interest in nutrition—he likes eating! As for shopping, he fills the grocery cart with three imported cheeses, an Italian salami and four packages of Twinkies. You can't let him near a food market. If this is the story of your life, you're going to have to handle the family program of sound nutrition yourself. Emily Shuman did.

FOODSTUFFS

Emily Shuman is an excellent cook and a careful shopper. She thrives on a sensible diet of big salads, fresh fruits and vegetables, chicken and fish, and being a person of moderation, only occasionally treats herself to a cheeseburger. Her husband, Martin (you met him in an earlier chapter), sleeps until noon and eats little all day until the cocktail hour when two or three drinks whet his appetite for the evening meal. He eats the nourishing, appetizing meal Emily has prepared, and soon after she retires for the night, he makes himself comfortable in front of the television set with his personal diet plan—ice cream, popcorn and nuts, a few beers and Heath bars. Martin nibbles away through the late-night programs. Martin is sedentary and he is plump and he doesn't seem to mind.

What has Emily done wrong? Not a thing. She's Martin's wife, not his mother. Emily provides well-balanced meals and Martin's supplemental grazing on junk food is his choice. Emily would prefer that Martin share her own sensible diet regimen, but she's not about to trade domestic tranquility for the role of a nagging wife.

FOOD NUTS

Jean Magnuson is a health food nut. Her husband has diabetes and a heart condition and she is religious about providing the right food for him. They eat no sugar, and junk food is absolutely prohibited. Jean calls junk food poison and has been known to go up to a complete stranger in the grocery store and tell him not to buy a particular product because he will be putting poison in his body. She is a controller and a caretaker. She monitors everything her husband eats, and he relies on her to keep him in good health.

Is Jean a better wife than Emily? Not necessarily. Jean's husband, Glenn, accepts her dedication to his well-being in the spirit it is offered, and he appreciates her concern. He would be surprised if anyone suggested that Jean was nagging.

HEN PECKS

Pat and Norman Gunn's friends dread their dinner dates together. Norman is on a special diet and his Pat is his custodian. As he orders she interrupts: "You can't have the chicken, Norman, it's fried," and then, in an aside to the waiter, "He'll have the fish and give him his salad without dressing." Later, when he goes to take a roll she literally slaps his hand. "No, no, no," she says. "No rolls and no butter."

Norman looks like he'd kill for a roll. Instead he puts a huge dollop of sour cream on his baked potato, looks at her, eyes blazing, and all but says, "What are you going to do about it?" Pat looks at him in disgust.

By this time everyone at the table is afraid to say anything, let alone eat anything. Pat is a nag and Norman is furious, and their friends can't wait to go home.

Helping each other stay on the straight and narrow is noble, but the effort can boomerang. So much depends on the spirit in which the help is given.

If you have to lose weight for health reasons, do you want your husband to remind you that you can't have the potatoes au gratin, or would his supervision make you so angry that you eat the potatoes and dessert as well? If he has to lose weight, ask him if he wants you to watch what he eats. If either of you wants to be an effective partner in a diet program, talk it over first and agree on how much monitoring each of you can accept from the other.

The subject of diet is a touchy one. It has all kinds of built-in traps. Have you ever found yourselves participants in dialogues similar to the following?

Entrapment

> HE: Why don't we try out that new Hungarian restaurant that just opened. The goulash is supposed to be terrific.
>
> SHE: Are you kidding! I can't eat goulash. It has a thousand calories.
>
> HE: Then let's try that Chinese place.
>
> SHE: Too salty. I hold water like a sponge.
>
> HE: How about McDonald's?
>
> SHE: You're always trying to do me in. You know I don't eat fast food.
>
> HE: Then make dinner.
>
> SHE: All you ever want me to do is slave in the kitchen.

Sabotage

> SHE: Let's go to the Chez Pierre. I hear the food is fabulous.
>
> HE: I don't know. The doctor says I should stay away from rich food. Isn't that food awfully high in cholesterol?

SHE: Oh, just a little won't hurt you. You can start on that diet tomorrow.

Compromise

HE: Let's go to that new Hungarian restaurant that just opened.

SHE: I'd love to, honey, but I'm afraid it wouldn't be very good for my health. Tell you what, why don't we go to the Seafood Shanty? You can get that lobster thermidor you like so much and I can have broiled fish. I'd really be grateful if you would.

While eating out can present a problem when you are on a special diet, you can be resourceful in making choices from the menu that are appropriate. Don't be afraid to ask that sauces be omitted and salad dressings be served on the side.

OPTIONS
DIETING UNDER GUARD

When Elizabeth Wendt's doctor told her she would need surgery to repair a blocked artery, she phoned her friend Ida, who had undergone the same surgical procedure the year before. "Ida warned me about the surgery. She told me that six or eight months after she had had the operation she still wasn't feeling well," Liz says, "so Ida went to the Pritikin Longevity Institute in California where she followed an intensive diet and exercise program with excellent results. Ida insisted I go there for an evaluation before I consented to having an operation."

Liz talked it over with her husband, Sherman, who had just retired. "Pritikin is extremely expensive—it was close to $7,000 for twenty-six days," she explains, "and we decided that instead of taking the usual grand tour of the world that so many couples do upon retirement, we would go to California together and I would check into the Pritikin Longevity Institute. It was the smartest thing I ever did.

"They scare you pretty good," she says. "The Pritikin regimen is boring and relentlessly rigid. It has more restrictions than permissions—no fat, no salt, no sugar, no caffeine. You learn that a regular exercise routine is as important as the diet itself, and the message is reinforced with a brainwashing lecture every evening after dinner.

"But it was worth it. I lost weight, felt stronger and healthier than I had in years and went home determined to control my physical problem with diet and exercise."

Once at home Liz found the extremely strict program difficult to follow, particularly since she had to cook for Sherman, too. However, her husband was so pleased with Liz's progress that he decided to go on the diet with her. "Sherm was wonderful," says Liz. "At first he went on the diet to give me moral support, but when he was able to go off all the medications he had been taking for gout and high blood pressure, he became a disciple. It's been an exciting success story for both of us for the past three years and I recommend it."

Although the Wendts have adhered to their diet for three years, it has not been easy. Liz admits she spends more time in the kitchen than she would like to, and they find themselves tempted to eat out more and more. "It's possible to eat out or even travel and still follow the Pritikin diet," she says, "but you have to take some foods with you. It is great having Sherm keep me company on the diet although when one of us backslides it doesn't take much for the other to follow. But then we try to help each other get our act together.

"One of the things the Pritikin people tell you is that eating is not an entertainment; it's only to provide fuel for your body." Liz pauses and shakes her head. "It's a great philosophy but it just isn't true. In our society dining is a major social event, but as long as Sherm and I work at it together we do pretty well."

DIETING BY THE BOOK

Barbara Nelson's husband, Willard, exercises a constant vigil over his weight, but recently it got away from him. A checkup by his doctor revealed that he had gained fourteen pounds and that his cholesterol level had gone up. His doctor recommended a diet high in complex carbohydrates and low in fat. Barbara bought a book on nutrition and together they mapped out an eating plan suited to their way of living. "We're not extreme at all," says Barbara. "We use little or no fat, we eat lots of fruits and vegetables; we stick to chicken and fish and, best of all, we eat bread and pasta, something we never allowed ourselves before."

The Nelsons have both lost a fair amount of weight and Willard feels better than he has in ages. He insists that he is eating more now than he used to when he was "dieting." The Nelsons don't consider themselves on a diet. They have just changed their eating habits, and they've done it together. They still enjoy an occasional cocktail and when they go to a restaurant, they order as close to their nutritional program as they can. On rare occasions they even order a dessert—they split it.

HELP

Dieting is boring. If either of you is on a diet for a specific health problem, or if you are just trying to lose or gain weight to satisfy your vanity, it helps to have at least tacit cooperation from your mate. Although the ultimate responsibility is with the individual dieter, there are ways in which you can help yourself, help each other and get valuable help from support groups.

It's never too late to educate yourself about good basic nutrition. When you were eighteen years old and wanted to squeeze into a dress for the weekend dance, you gave up food altogether or ate nothing but water-melon or lived on celery and carrots. Today your digestive system rebels at such maltreatment. It is far wiser to make sure that your diet contains the four basic food groups and that you cut down on fats, salt and sugar. We no longer can tolerate the ravaging effects of fad diets.

When eating out you can order your broiled fish un-salted; you can request your Chinese food be free of MSG. In many retirement communities local Chinese restaurants do not use MSG at all and make sure their patrons know it.

There are numerous books on the subject of nutrition. Jane Brody writes regularly about it in *The New York Times*. We recommend her book *Jane Brody's Nutrition Book* (Bantam) and Jane Fonda's book *Women Coming of Age* (Simon & Schuster) as well.

If you feel the need for supervision, even if it's only that of your peers, Weight Watchers offers a sound, supervised nutritional program. Overeaters Anonymous is an excellent organization particularly suited to people who see their weight problem as an addiction. If you are a chocoholic, a compulsive overeater, if you find that you are literally obsessed about food—that diet, your weight, what you're going to eat next occupies too much of your time and attention—the Overeaters Anonymous program might be the one for you. If you and your husband *both* have weight problems, go on one of these programs together. It can be a constructive retirement project.

If he refuses, don't blame your failure to lose weight on him. Ultimately only you are the one responsible for your own well-being, as he is for maintaining his own good health.

KEEP MOVING AND STAY FIT

Joan Harrison's husband, Mike, tries to jog five miles every day. He says it makes him feel good and helps him keep his weight down. "It's a good thing he doesn't rely on me for encouragement. It's up to him to discipline himself," says Joan. "It's the same with vitamin pills—he lines up all the vitamin bottles every morning before breakfast. I probably should take vitamins, too, but I don't bother. Laziness. I don't run if I can walk; I don't walk if I can drive to my destination."

Joan is one of the few women in her circle of friends who isn't into some structured exercise regimen. "I've made a number of starts," she says, "even bought a stationary bicycle, but my good intentions came crashing around me after a week or two because it was *so* boring. I do worry about me. I vow to find an exercise program for myself every time I run for a bus and find myself gasping for air, my heart racing, after ten or fifteen steps.

"I rationalize that walking to the grocery store, doing some limited housework equates exercise. Then I rationalize further when I consider that my mother, who didn't move very fast either, lived until 84. But I'm envious of the fun I'm missing. Tennis and golf are socializing activities as well as good for one's general health. Even a regular program of swimming at the Y would give me a sense of accomplishment. Sometimes I think I have no character. My enthusiasm for the aerobics class, the bicycle, a mandatory daily hike fizzles after a couple of weeks."

Joan was delighted when she heard that Dr. Christine Friedman of the Lifeline Adult Fitness Program at the University of Southern Maine recommends a brisk thirty-minute walk three times a week as a prescription for a reasonable exercise program. Convinced that she had found a schedule that even she could follow, Joan made a date with her neighbor Debby to set out on a walk together every Monday, Wednesday and Friday. Because she has someone to walk with she has stayed with this nondemanding exercise program. "I like to think of it as progress," says Joan. "If I drop out of this I'm a failure only three times a week instead of every day."

WALK FOR YOUR LIFE

Do you recognize Joan? If you're inclined to identify with her you'd better get moving. According to Dr. Friedman, thirty minutes of brisk walking three times a week can be a lifetime program that almost anyone can follow. She advises that you check with your personal physician before starting on any formal exercise program, or a program of your own design. Dr. Friedman, who works with people recovering from coronary and pulmonary illnesses, recommends a five-minute warm-up walk, then thirty minutes of brisk walking to raise the heart rate, followed by a five-minute cooldown stroll. For those of you who have been sedentary in recent years, she cautions that you start your fitness program gradually, walking briskly for nine minutes the first week, ten minutes the second, eleven the third week until you reach your goal of thirty minutes of brisk walking three times a week.

Now that you've made up your mind to follow Dr. Friedman's advice, you'd like to get your husband out of his easy chair, too. So you announce enthusiastically, "Honey, we're really going to get in shape. We're going to go for a walk this morning." And he says:

"I can't walk, my toe hurts," or

"I can't walk, I have to read the paper," or

"I can't walk, I don't have walking shoes," or

"I can't walk, I have to wash the car, call my broker and write my will."

You have two choices. The first is subterfuge. Betty Jean Browning got her husband out on the road by canceling their subscription to the *Los Angeles Times*. The nearest newsstand is over a mile away. Dean

Browning, an avid reader of the *Times*, reluctantly agreed to walk with her every morning to get the paper. He has learned to enjoy the walk and he feels his endurance has improved. "I do give in one day a week," says Betty Jean. "The Sunday paper is delivered and we read it in bed. I couldn't ask Dean to walk carrying ten pounds of paper. Have you ever seen the size of the Sunday L.A. *Times*?"

The second choice you have is to go it alone. Face the fact that your husband only uses his feet to press the brake and the accelerator in his car. Buy a small radio with earphones, or use the time to listen to your own thoughts and set out on your morning walk. You deserve to be fit.

Fortunately, most people aren't as sedentary as Joan Harrison or Dean Browning. The majority of the women we interviewed led physically active lives and depended on regular exercise for a sense of well-being. Many of them play tennis or golf, swim or jog.

Generally, husbands pursue their own exercise programs separately. But there are those couples who do rely on each other as playmates.

THEY EXERCISE TOGETHER

The Raneys, who are in their seventies and live in a retirement village, always play golf together. Their nine holes three or four times a week seem to be just right for them.

Art Fletcher is a retired golf professional. His wife, Carol, has become a top golfer and club champ, and not just by osmosis. She and Art have their separate golf dates, but about once a week they are out on the course together.

Doris and Alfred Harris go to Aspen every year. He loves to ski and she joins him when he's had his fill of the slopes and they cross-country ski together.

Jean Magnuson, who watches her husband's diet so closely, also sees to it that he gets his exercise. They

enjoy playing indoor tennis together in a mixed doubles
game once a week, and they do walk together. But Jean
has an amazing exercise program of her own, and for
very good reason. She has a common but severe problem, osteoarthritis.

As with every cause that she embraces, Jean sets
the rules and then she abides by them religiously. She
awakens early and does gentle stretching exercises,
including working the fingers of each hand until they
are warm and supple. She then dresses appropriately
(warm clothing as soon as there's a chill in the air, light
clothing for the summer months) and heads out for the
trail where she jogs for two miles. She does not find
jogging hard on her joints. She plays in a regular tennis
game all year long and in the late afternoon or early
evening does yoga exercises which are relaxing and
also keep her limber. "I'm afraid if I don't keep moving
I'll just freeze in one place," says Jean. Jean is fighting
a daily battle with her arthritic condition and her de-
termination is her greatest asset.

IT MAKES GOOD SENSE

Be aware of your need for exercise. Remember:
  • If you and your husband keep moving you can be
    sure all of your parts will work better.
  • If both of you engage in regular aerobic exercise
    (walking briskly three times a week is a minimum
    goal) you'll improve your cardiovascular system.
    (*Note*: If you don't live in the Sun Belt, winter
    walking can be done in shopping malls. Many malls
    open their doors at 7:30 a.m. even though the stores
    do not open until 10 a.m., just so local exercisers
    can take advantage of the interior heated space.)
  • Exercise relieves stress and lifts depression; it even
    improves sleep. Both you and your retired husband
    would do better to bicycle than to pop sleeping pills.
  • Enjoy exercise! It's recreational and it's social. You'll
    meet people at the tennis courts or at the health

club. Engaging in physical activity gives life zest and makes you feel young.

IT'S ONLY A GAME

You tried and you failed.

If you started a yoga class and found that you were bored to death, or you bought Jane Fonda's exercise tape and realized you couldn't have followed it at 20 years old, let alone now, don't give up on exercise. You have just chosen the wrong activity.

Dr. Friedman warns that setting fitness goals that are inappropriate can be self-defeating. Take up tennis, but forget Wimbledon. If you enjoy walking, don't feel you must run. Few people stick with a physical activity from which they don't get some pleasure.

If athletic games and physical fitness activities bore you, you probably enjoy social interaction more. Go walking with your husband or with a friend or two. You'll be so busy talking—exercising your jaw—you won't notice you're exercising your body at the same time. If you find you get too winded to talk when you walk, all the more reason to exercise.

A LIFT FOR YOUR SPIRIT

So you've stuck to your diet. And you've worked your body into tip-top shape, but there are those wrinkles around your eyes, and the laugh lines around your mouth aren't funny any more. If you are like most women you slap on a little extra moisturizer and let it go at that. Marilyn Biondi is grateful because her husband thinks she looks so well. Says Marilyn, "Just when gravity has made my skin collapse, my husband's eyes have aged and he doesn't see a line in my face."

Carol Fletcher didn't feel that way. Years in the California sun had carved deep lines in her beautiful face. She opted for a face-lift and a skin peel. Carol looks better than ever—not necessarily younger, but extremely well for her age.

Plastic surgery, contact lenses, capped teeth—take advantage of them if they make you feel better about yourself. But don't count on these changes to solve deep-seated problems. If the bags under your eyes really bother you, start your research. Talk to your own personal physician. Get his or her opinion. If he feels you are a qualified candidate for plastic surgery, he will recommend a qualified surgeon. (No cut-rate cutting here, please!) Feeling good about the way you look is very much a part of your personal health.

ALCOHOL: USE AND ABUSE

When the clock strikes four, Susan and Stewart Ecklund join each other for an afternoon cocktail. When it strikes five, Susan knows it's time to go into the kitchen and start dinner. The Ecklunds rarely dine out. Stewart takes little or no interest in cooking, so for forty-plus years Susan has been hitting the kitchen at five every evening to make dinner. Lately Susan has been hitting something else, too: she's been hitting the bottle. "I have a bad case of kitchenitis," says Susan. "I have to take two stiff drinks just to be able to face making dinner. I'm a little worried. I've never felt the need for liquor to get through something before."

After forty years of the same routine we wouldn't blame Susan if she drank all the cooking sherry. But wouldn't it be wise if Susan made some changes in her life? Doesn't she deserve to "retire" too?

While everyone frets about the increase in teenage drinking, not much is said about another group that is also imbibing alcohol—older men and women. Is there a connection between retirement and increased alcohol consumption? For some of our interviewees, it would seem so.

Sylvia and Ted Fitzsimmons visited Mexico half a dozen times during their married life and seriously considered moving there after Ted's retirement. They had heard of a colony of retired North Americans in Mexico, so they packed their bags and set off to investigate. "You can't generalize about retired people. Retirement is exactly what each couple makes it, but when we settled in for an extended visit we were surprised to learn that the permanent residents who had lived there for years never ventured out of the retirement compound to meet their Mexican neighbors," says Sylvia. "From the retirees we met, we got the impression that the main intellectual activity is a running game of bridge and the high point of the day was the happy hour when many of them would get sloshed for the evening." The Fitzsimmons decided not to retire to Mexico.

Sylvia's observation seems extreme. There's nothing about retirement that will make a person an alcoholic. However, there is something about retirement which can cause a person with a predisposition to alcoholism to become more and more dependent on liquor. Gwen Porter can testify to that.

Gwen Porter's husband, Mike, retired three years ago from a high-powered job with an international conglomerate. He is a hearty and gregarious man who traveled a lot and was exceptionally good in his relationships with other people. In Mike's position he often wined and dined customers, and he had ample opportunity to become more than a social drinker. Although he drank a good deal, he never felt he was in any way an alcoholic. After all, he was very successful, a good family man and a stable person.

Mike was an ardent fisherman, but after retirement, having all the time in the world, Mike found fishing less appealing than before. He tried tennis and he took up golf, but he isn't a competitive athlete and he doesn't feel deeply attached to either sport. Gwen is worried about him. "Having too little to do makes him edgy as a cat," she says.

"Mike's drinking increased after his retirement. It was boredom. After a man retires he doesn't hear from the men he used to have lunch with," says Gwen.

Mike became a sipper. He always had a drink nearby and sipped it almost all day long, just enough to feel relaxed, to feel the glow. "He never was really drunk," says Gwen. What went wrong?

First of all, Mike's blood pressure took a quantum jump into the stratosphere and his doctor prescribed medication. He made no mention of his drinking to his physician because he denied it to himself. He also was told to lose weight, which puzzled Mike because he was a moderate eater. It was alcohol that had bloated him and added calories. Mike's health continued to deteriorate and he found it necessary to undergo a thorough examination in a well-known clinic. It was there that he was told that his liver had become enlarged. There was no question; Mike's alcohol consumption had now seriously affected his health.

"I can't tell you how shocked we were," says Gwen. It has taken her some time to concede that he is an alcoholic. "He never acted like an alcoholic, or at least like some I've seen. He really was a very good drinker. He held his liquor well."

Mike was forced to face his problem when his doctor warned him about the consequences. "I really craved it, I had a bad time," says Mike. "You know what it's like here in Scottsdale. You don't just go out to dinner, you go to someone's home first for drinks. Then it's on to the restaurant and another round or two of drinks. It drives me up the wall; sometimes it's two hours of drinking before we eat."

At this point Gwen stepped in and took charge. Now when friends make a date with the Porters to go to dinner, Gwen asks that there be no long cocktail hour. Everyone meets at a relatively early hour at the restaurant. Mike doesn't mind if others have a drink, but dinner is ordered at the same time. Mike has been fairly successful in overcoming his alcohol abuse but each day presents a struggle. His major interest now is working on improving his health. Once he feels better he plans to invest in a small business. He doesn't want to go back to work full-time, but he feels the need to be busy and to fill his day with something more than tennis and golf and drinking.

WHAT ABOUT YOU?

Have you noticed that you and your husband have taken to starting the cocktail hour earlier and earlier? Do you find that alcohol is necessary when you get together with your friends? Do you find that your intake of liquor has increased dramatically, or that your husband's has?

As we grow older our tolerance for alcohol grows less. We're more likely to suffer headaches, hangovers and real digestive problems from what we once considered moderate amounts of alcohol.

Les Manley, a moderate drinker who has always liked Scotch, now gets violent migraine headaches from his favorite drink. Leona Perry gets severe reactions to red and white wine. Both of them were able to moderate their drinking habits, but there are people who drink despite the pain, wanting that immediate glow and denying the resulting misery.

If you and your husband do not have a history of alcoholism, you probably can cut down or cut out without too much trouble. But if you find that your husband is drinking far too much and refuses to face it, don't nag. Don't become a scolding parent to his bad little boy. If you do, your relationship will be in serious trouble. Alcoholics thrive on being told they are naughty children. They take scoldings because they feel their worthlessness, but they also feel that once having been punished they can imbibe again.

If discussing his drinking habits with your husband as one adult to another does not work, we suggest that you seek help at your local Alanon group. Yes, we said *you* go. Your husband will not go to Alcoholics Anonymous just because you ask him to; he'll go when he feels he must. But if *you* are having difficulty with his problem, then Alanon is the place to find out what to do about it. It is an amazingly successful organization, and if you give it a chance, it will help you get insight into your problems. And you're worth being helped.

If you know deep in your heart that you are the one who is abusing alcohol and all of your resolutions to stop just don't work, get out the phone book and look up the number of your local Alcoholics Anonymous chapter. Though AA is not the only organization dedicated to treating alcohol abuse, it is one of the most successful. Don't judge AA by the first meeting. Give it at least six weeks and then decide. Few people leave if they are able to stick out the six-week trial period.

More and more hospitals are dealing with the problem of alcohol addiction. Many have excellent treatment centers. For example, Lutheran General Hospital in Park Ridge, Illinois, not only treats the alcoholic but works with the members of his or her family as well.

The key word in dealing with alcoholism is honesty. Before you can do a thing about it, you have to admit that there is a problem, and that's the first step on the road to recovery.

A KEY TO LONGEVITY

A drink with friends, a quiet cocktail with your husband, is one of the enjoyments of civilized life. In fact, a small amount of alcohol each day is actually good for the circulation.

Have you heard about the Abkhazians, a community of Russian peasants who have a life expectancy well past 100 years? Contrary to claims by the yogurt industry, it's not their daily consumption of yogurt that keeps Abkhazian doctors at bay. *Aging* magazine reports that scientists at a Soviet-American symposium on longevity research noted that climbing the steep terrain of their mountain villages provides continuous exercise for the cardiovascular systems of Abkhazian women and men. Their diet is wholesome but not unusual: they consume limited protein and eat mainly vegetables, beans, sour milk products and honey. Neither the Abkhazian elderly nor their families expect the later years of life to be spent in poor health.

Oh yes, they also consume substantial quantities of wine.

PASS THE PILLS

Our generation into drug abuse? No way! LSD, heroin, marijuana, even cocaine—that's for younger people with bad habits and money to burn. But we beg to differ. Our generation does have a problem with drugs, drugs our doctors prescribe for us, over-the-counter drugs and pills we pass around to each other.

Terry Strang's doctor is an understanding fellow. He knew the strain she was under when her elderly father was ill and her mother, a stroke victim, was unable to care for him. Her husband was having trouble adjusting to retirement and her oldest son's marriage looked like it was going on the rocks. Her doctor gave her a prescription for Valium. Her gynecologist was sympathetic too when she told him she couldn't sleep. He gave her a prescription for Dalmane.

Terry was on her way. Through careful planning and downright manipulation of several doctors, she managed to keep a constant supply of tranquilizers and barbiturates on hand.

As pressures grew and time passed, Terry became more and more dependent on the drugs. In short, she had a habit. Unfortunately, she also used alcohol to get her through social situations, and it wasn't long before she displayed symptoms of disorientation and, finally, an incapacity to function. Neither Terry nor her husband could accept the fact that she was an addict. People like the Strangs—upper-middle-class, retired, solid citizens, good parents—don't become drug-addicted. At least they think they don't.

Terry had to be hospitalized and it was in the hospital that her dependency was recognized and a course of medical and psychiatric treatment was initiated.

WARNING: Socially acceptable drugs, drugs prescribed by well-meaning doctors, have to be taken with care. Do you go to an orthopedist for your tennis elbow, to your internist for an annual checkup, to your gynecologist for a six-month examination, and are you getting medication from all three of them? Do you keep them informed of all the drugs you are taking? If you don't, you are taking dangerous chances. Be sure your doctor knows what medications you are taking that *he* (or *she*) has *not* prescribed!

SHARING

The strongest pain relievers in Carol and Art Fletcher's medicine cabinet are aspirin and Alka-Seltzer. But one day Art got a sore throat and complained about it to his neighbor Clarence. Clarence has a small pharmacy in his own home; he seems to save all the drugs ever prescribed for him. Clarence not only suggested an antibiotic, he supplied Art with penicillin he had on the shelf. If you have a sore shoulder, he'll give you some Indocin, an anti-inflammatory drug.

Clarence is a menace. He has not caused a major tragedy yet, mostly because people decline his offers, but wait until he prescribes an antibiotic for someone with a drug allergy. *Whatever you and your husband do, don't share drugs with friends or with each other.* The anti-inflammatory your husband takes for his bad back might make you violently ill when you take it for your sore knee.

SLEEPING

Do you have to take a sleeping pill before you can get to sleep at night? Does the anticipation of a bad night's sleep distress you even before your head hits the pillow? Accept the fact that your body no longer needs eight hours of uninterrupted sleep every night. You may have to get up once or twice to stumble to the bathroom. And if you awake at 6 a.m. when you no longer have to get up that early—after all, your husband is retired and doesn't have to make the 8:08—don't fret. Get up and enjoy the morning hours. Take a walk, get in some reading.

AND SO TO BED

Chances are you and your retired husband share a moment of envy when you read of octogenarian couples who still enjoy active sex lives after half a century or more of marriage. You may both still be on the sunny side of 60 and wondering where the fire went. Was it those few extra pounds (yours or his) that came between you? Do you suspect you are no longer sexually attractive to him; is he no longer sexually attractive to you? Are you both too blasé, too settled in, too bored to try something new?

Sex therapists tell us that the most important factors in sustaining an active sex life is a reasonable state of good health and a sexually interesting and interested partner. Sex therapy pioneers Masters and Johnson say: "Even if they are healthy participants in a warm, secure relationship, sexual effectiveness does not ensue as an automatic reward to... an aging partnership. A mutually stimulating sexual relationship needs care and feeding by both partners in any age group... and it's particularly true in later life."[*] The Masters and Johnson research team claims sexual boredom may be the greatest detriment to the effectiveness of sexual interaction between men and women in any long-standing relationship.

Florence and Peter Quinn's sexual reawakening came

[*]*Sex and the Aging Process.* The Edward Henderson Award Lecture, 38th annual meeting of the American Geriatric Society, Boston, April 30, 1981.

in the guise of late-night movies. "When cable television came to Hillside I found my husband interested in the worst garbage, honestly," says Florence. "There's *Emmanuelle* and all those movies. We don't go to the movies much, so I enjoy watching reruns on TV that I have missed in the last years. But Peter and I watch television at different times. I watch my movies and go to bed early because I get up early to get out and do things. He gets up in time for lunch. So anyway, he watches cable later. I don't know, it seems to be a sexual thing, watching this stuff, like a vicarious thrill. Our sex life had dwindled greatly. Cable has certainly made it livelier—it still isn't very lively—but we do enjoy the stimulation of the very erotic things that are on cable."

"Our sexual interludes have been fewer and farther between times," says Maude Greene. "Our sex life sort of tapered off, but we never discuss it. After being married for so many years we know each other, we know we love each other, and the change in the nature of our sexual activities doesn't present a major problem."

One therapist we interviewed observed, "I think there's a high degree of companionate marriage. I think a companionate type of marriage is perfectly valid among older people."

Marge Moore, on the other hand, can pinpoint the exact moment her sexual relationship with her husband ground to a halt. "It was on June 7, 1982," she says, "the day I joined NOW."

Dr. William H. Masters points out, "When any physiologic alterations in sexual response become obvious in [the wife's] male partner, her initial reaction may be to question her own sexuality. His obvious slow erective response may be interpreted as a loss of interest in her. If he doesn't ejaculate regularly, she may be concerned that he doesn't need her or," says Masters, "she may fear he has some new sexual interest."

Most times these fears are unfounded. Feeling guilty about your husband's reduced sexual drive can be counterproductive. Chances are he feels the loss as much as you do. It would be wise to take these possibilities into consideration: If your husband is taking medication, particularly diuretics for high blood pressure, his sexual capacity can be greatly diminished. Don't put additional pressure on your husband by criticizing him for not fulfilling your sexual needs. If he has to be on medication which interferes with his sexual performance, be understanding. Be innovative.

If he's using alcohol in order to psych himself into the mood for love he may, in truth, be psyching himself into impotence. A glass of wine or a cocktail can be a lovely relaxant, but as little as two bar drinks reduce blood circulation to a degree that could have a disastrous effect on a man's ability to perform sexually. If alcohol is interfering with his sexual performance tell him you want to make love and ask him not to drink. If that fails, approach him at a time of day when he has not been drinking. That's what's so lovely about retirement.

As we said in Chapter 3, "Doing Things Together," sexual intercourse is not the only way to show love and affection. Exchanging loving words, being physically close, just fondling and touching each other can be deeply satisfying.

Romantic reticence on her husband's part is not one of Louise Wescott's problems. "Before he retired from thirty years with the city police force, Grant often worked nights and I worked days," Louise says. "That was a schedule I could deal with in our thirty-four years of marriage. Grant's sexual appetite always surpassed mine. Now that he's retired, he has more opportunities to prove himself in bed, and I spend the train ride home from work each day devising schemes to divert his attention.

"Grant has latched onto two buddies who are also retired. They spend most of their days together, which is a mixed blessing, because he brags about his sexual exploits to anyone who will listen. I know my personal life is no longer personal. Grant has a lot of energy. He had been looking forward to retirement and has been resourceful in finding things to do. But his greatest preoccupation is with his performance in bed. If I beg off, his feelings are hurt. He wants my complete attention when I'm home, which is something new. On one hand, he says he appreciates me more; on the other, he never wants to be alone and his demands on my time overwhelm me. I have always enjoyed my time alone—to read a book, or write letters. Now I use visits with my married daughter as an escape hatch." She laughs. "I even suggested that he find a girlfriend, but he took me seriously and there, I did it again. I hurt his feelings."

Retirement seems to be the catalyst for Grant's increased sexual demands. Feeling a sudden loss of identity, he wants to prove that he hasn't lost his masculinity as well. Louise will have to be patient and supportive, but it's not necessary that she acquiesce to his every demand. There are ways that Louise can say no without withdrawing her affection from him. She can reassure him that she does love him, and, if she's smart, when she says no to him on Friday night, she can make a date with him for Saturday morning. Letting your husband know that he's still the man in your life even though you don't want to make love at that moment is important. Making a definite date with him for later is even better.

Sexuality was not an overriding problem with the majority of women we spoke to. While some of the women were unwilling to volunteer information about their sexual relationship with their husband, many did respond to direct questions on the subject. What became apparent was that in these marriages of many years a compatible and acceptable sexual relationship had developed. Out of the seventy-five women we interviewed, only four expressed dissatisfaction with their sexual lives with their husbands.

POSTRETIREMENT BLUES

Quite a few of the wives interviewed reported that shortly after retirement their husbands started to have physical and emotional symptoms they had not exhibited before. They complained of fatigue, a variety of aches and pains and were often moody and withdrawn. "It can't be stress, he has so little pressure on him now," said one woman. "He complained less when he was working sixty hours a week. Now that he has time he complains constantly."

Postretirement depression is not an uncommon syndrome, so don't be surprised if you notice changes in your husband's moods. Most of the husbands who suffered from these emotional ups and downs recovered within a year of their retirement. Only a few of the wives said that their husbands sought professional therapy. What you do is listen! He will need to talk about his feelings, and remember, you are his closest friend. Be patient. Be affectionate. Be supportive. Be aware you cannot solve his problem for him.

Our research for this book has led us to the conclusion that support groups for retired people might be extremely useful. At present few, if any, such groups exist. Senior centers do bring retired people together for meetings about estate planning and current events, but retired couples might benefit from meetings that deal with the problems and adjustments of retirement.

Since women are far better at networking than men, it seems to us that support groups for wives of retirees might be an excellent first step. That is why we invited ten wives of retired men to participate in two discussion groups and to share their trials and their triumphs.

9
HERE'S TO THE LADIES WHO LUNCH

In conducting the interviews for our book, we were struck by the number of women who felt isolated in their situations. It was not uncommon to hear a woman say, "I know I must be the only one who feels like this, but sometimes I have to get away from my husband," or "I know my story is unique, but I'm going back to work now that he's home."

Thus we got the idea that it might be interesting to bring a group of women together, all wives of retirees, for an afternoon luncheon and some straight talk. We wanted to see if they would share their experiences about the problems of retirement as well as their successes. Since the women whose stories are in this book are from every part of the country, we decided it would be even more interesting to have two such luncheons, one in the bustling northern urban area of Chicago and one in Indian Wells, California, a small, sunny retirement community in the vicinity of Palm Springs. Our goal was to compare and contrast the concerns of the women from each of these geographic areas.

Is the quality of retirement life different for women who remain in the same location where their husbands worked and they raised their children than it is for those who migrated to the Sun Belt, where many of their neighbors are also newcomers? Are there differences between the interests of women living in a city with populations diverse in age, ethnicity and economic background and those of women now living in a more stratified setting where people are inclined to be somewhat similar? Another reason for these get-togethers was that we wanted to see if these women, most of whom did not know each other, would be willing to share their experiences.

It was suggested by two of the professionals we interviewed, one a marriage and family therapist and the other a psychoanalyst, that support groups for retirees and wives of retirees could be highly beneficial. We do not suggest that these first meetings were pilot meetings for a support program, but they did demonstrate that women by nature are able to communicate with each other at personal levels. The subjects touched on were personal identity, adjustment in marriage, age, friendship, health and finances—not bad for a first time get-together.

On a crisp fall Chicago afternoon five women whose husbands are retired joined us for lunch. None of the five women had met each other before. However, it took very little prompting on our part to get them to share their experiences. If you're like us, you should enjoy eavesdropping on what they had to say over the chicken salad.

*I*ntroducing:

• *Irene.* Irene's husband is a retired Internal Revenue Service agent. She was a social worker who retired two years after her husband did. She does volunteer work two days a week.

• *Norma.* Norma's husband is a retired manufacturer. She was active in her husband's business and continues to keep their financial records and do their taxes.

- *Doris*. Doris's husband retired from his seat on the Chicago Board of Trade. At present she is the publisher and editor of a literary magazine.
- *Emily*. Emily's husband is a retired soft-drink bottler. She is an athletic woman who plays tennis, hikes, tap dances and claims she is saving golf for her old age.
- *Jill*. Jill's husband is a retired retailer. They have been married fifteen years. Jill was widowed when she was 31 and at that time became a full-time practicing psychotherapist.

These are their exact words:

IRENE: What am I doing now? Nothing. But looking back I am doing the things that are interesting to me. I've always been interested in the ACLU so I volunteered for two days a week. What it does for me is that when I'm dissatisfied with the political situation, saying I'm upset and what can I do, I feel I'm doing something. You feel less frustrated when you have a mode of activity, so I do that.

DORIS: Right now I'm publishing and editing a literary magazine. Nonprofit, natch! We're launching a magazine of fresh, diverse short stories. It's a line of work I've been in, on another publication, for about ten years. So I'm experienced. I enjoy it. I think it's insanity because it requires the energy I had ten years ago. Now I'm scared. I want to make this thing go. It's not the lack of ideas—it's the energy thing. It's going to be a small-circulation magazine; it's not *The New Yorker*. It's a labor of love.

NORMA: Does your husband have any part in it?

DORIS: A minor part. He's designing the graphics and keeping the books.

EMILY: I'm poles apart. I mainly enjoy physical things. I do like to read and I like bridge but I like physical activity. The energy you talk about—I have an excess. I take no credit for it, it's innate.

JILL: I'm a full-time-and-a-half practicing psychotherapist and there's nothing in the world I would rather do. I do it with a passion that sometimes runs me. I think I have a mission. Although I see fewer couples and individuals now, I do a lot more teaching and training. All someone has to do is say to me, "Come to some desert island with about twelve people who would like growth in their professional life," and he can have me, morning, noon and night.

EMILY: My husband retired four years ago. We talked about his retirement a year or two before he retired. Knowing I'm such a physically active person, I had real trepidations about it. I thought, my God, what will I do? But my husband kept assuring me I should go about my own business as I always have done. He said his retirement should have no bearing on my program, on anything I wanted to do.

NORMA: Did it work out that way?

EMILY: My husband is a night person and I'm a day person. He doesn't want breakfast and he doesn't want lunch and if he does, he prefers to make it on his own. We're together for dinner. As physically active as I am, that's how perfectly sedentary he is. He sleeps late in the day, he goes to bed late at night. He reads or watches some stupid thing on television until all hours, so when he wakes up at least half the day is gone for me. We do spend time together with our grandchildren. And luckily, we do that fairly often.

IRENE: The I.R.S. offered my husband early retirement. He always had many interests—music, art, woodwork. I was working, and after his retirement I wanted to stay on my job and I did. It worked out pretty well; the only differences we had—he moved lock, stock and barrel into the house, and he was going to run things his way. It was all right while I was still working, but when I stopped it was difficult moving back into position again.

JILL: Four years ago my husband, who is a businessman, retired. He is as active now as he was before, working with the Executive Service Corps, which is for retired businessmen. He adores it. He's a few years older than I am. He's the most sensible thing in my life. Things we were both upset about twelve years ago we can laugh about now. Have a few good giggles. At one time things were much more important than they are now because we're both very stubborn people. He had been married to his first wife thirty-one years. She was a traditional homemaker—different from me in every way, shape or form. I had lived alone for fifteen years; I didn't have to be accountable to anyone but me. The tasks were new for both of us. It was exciting—it had a lot of electricity.

DORIS: Interesting observation, that the trials of adjustment and the abrasions can also be exciting.

JILL: I think what both of us knew was that neither one of our survivals depended upon this adjustment. We knew enough about ourselves as people to know survival had nothing to do with it. There was no great risk.

DORIS: My husband "changed vocations"—at least that's the way we put it because as my friend's sister-in-law once said, "You don't say 'retirement'; there's a pejorative feeling about the word. Say 'changed vocations.'"

IRENE: When you retire you become a nonentity. People identify you by what you do rather than who you are. If you just say you're retired, you're a nothing. I heard about an in-depth study on doctors who retire—how they go from being the great gods to becoming nothing.

DORIS: Well, my husband, in his early fifties, became an architect. He went back to school for five years. He always wanted to be an architect when he grew up. He was on the Board of Trade—a gambler, as his father was before him. He hated every minute of it but he was there for thirty years. Finally, when he came out a little ahead—or we did—we talked it over and I said, "I think we'll both live longer if we quit while we're ahead."

IRENE: He changed jobs; he didn't really retire?

DORIS: He's a very active, pragmatic fellow. He wasn't going to sit home and read books. He's always wanted to be an architect and it was a rigorous program.

IRENE: Can you imagine going back to school in your fifties and taking things like calculus and statistics?

DORIS: It was the long hours, the staying up all

night that the architecture students, like the medical students, do. In other words, breaking your back over that drafting board. That is taxing. His fellow students were in their late twenties. I became the housemother; they treated him not as an older fellow but as a contemporary colleague. That part of it for him was lovely. But the physical task was very difficult. It's hard enough to concentrate on any intellectual pursuit, but for this one I had to say, "Thank God for his health."

EMILY: Did you encourage him?

DORIS: I certainly did; it was a full-time job.

NORMA: I am really someone my husband can always talk to about whether to do this project or that project. He sold his manufacturing business in 1967, at which time, in the eyes of the world, he had retired because he didn't have to go to the office. He had always managed to have his factory close enough to home to come home to lunch. He is not interested in sports, no card playing. He ran into trouble in later years when his friends retired. They wanted him to go to lunch or go to the senior center, things he considers to be a waste of time. He has his office at home—runs his real estate from there. It's enough to keep him busy and to have contact with other people. He can go on trips, but he doesn't want to. He just wants to be home. His being home all the time began to be hard to take. If you're together all the time doing things, there's nothing to talk about because it's happening to both of you. Maybe in self-defense, I went back to school.

EMILY: What did you study?

NORMA: I always wanted to teach art but art teachers are a dime a dozen. They did need math teachers so I boned up on that. While I was teaching I got a master's degree, and I also teach weaving. Weaving has been a hobby with me since the early '40s. If you do it long enough you've met most of the problems, so I have become an expert.

EMILY: Doris, when you go to a party and someone says, "What do you do?" do you like to say, "I'm editing a magazine"?

DORIS: I used to like to say that—it carried me a long way. The main thing is it keeps me busy. I feel I'm involved in a positive way. I'm excited about something. I have a passion. It's not that I love editing, but I think it is something I feel good about. Before I decided on this new magazine, I thought, should I go on with my own writing? What should I do? I'm glad I made the decision, but I've become snappish since I've become involved again in the magazine. Our moods don't mesh as well. You need infinite patience in establishing new boundaries. But it does get better.

JILL: If he feels excluded in decision making, my husband pouts. These things take on new importance in retirement.

IRENE: My husband procrastinates when he doesn't want to do something I want. If I get annoyed, I leave the house. He didn't want drapes on the windows. When I ordered them they lay around the house for six months before he put them up. I couldn't hire someone else to put them up because he is always around.

NORMA: The stress stopped in our home when the kids left home. Our major disagreements were on how to handle the kids. But women live someone else's life most of their lives, their children's, their husband's. My inclination is to go along with my husband, rather than create a stir.

EMILY: Someone once told me at a bridge game that she had to leave early to make dinner for her husband. The minute your husband leaves in the morning, set the table. No matter when he comes home it looks as if you have just been preparing for him. And I was just thinking, now that our husbands are home all the time, we can't do that.

IRENE: When I was younger I may have been dogmatic, but I was much more interested and tolerant of people who were a lot different from me. People who might have been the lunatic fringe, the crazies. I could put up with a lot because those kind of people interested me. Now that I'm older I'm unwilling to put the time in. Relationships with these people are a lot of hard work. Now when I meet some of these people later in life, those flaky people I would have had unlimited time for, I'm no longer interested.

JILL: If you haven't gotten more discriminating, that's when you have a real problem. I must tell you that over the years I've gotten much clearer on what's shit and what's shinola.

When asked if they felt they could talk to their women friends more frankly than to their husbands, the answers were unanimous.

JILL: I'm more willing to discuss my physical

self with a woman friend. It disturbs my husband. Not that he won't listen, but if there's something wrong with me, he gets upset. If I want to speculate—what do you think this is, or what are my feelings—I go to one of my woman friends. I don't keep it from my husband, but I think I am *heard* differently by another woman.

DORIS: When there's something really on my mind, when I'm really upset, I find it difficult to open up except to another woman—to specific women with whom I am close.

JILL: I have very dear friends who are women. Over the years I have let go of old, old friendships for I have changed, my interests have changed.

NORMA: I think that husbands, at times, are very intolerant of their wives' infirmities. If I should come down with the flu, he wouldn't even think of offering a cup of tea. My friends have the same situation. Husbands just do not reciprocate the nurturing care.

IRENE: If I'm sick my husband says, "You don't have to cook dinner, just make me a sandwich." Men are very impatient. When you try to have a discussion on the level of what you're feeling, they get impatient, if not downright frightened. If I say to him, "Let me tell you how I really feel," he freezes.

JILL: I was sitting in the bathtub the other morning and my husband was shaving and I said to him, "I have the funniest feeling—like I'm waiting for something. I can't tell you what it is, but I think something is going to happen." "What are you waiting for?" he asked. "I really don't know what it is—like something *intangible* is going to happen." Well, he couldn't figure it out, and for the life of me I couldn't make him understand.

IRENE: When you try to talk to men about something that's going to happen, it gets removed to another level. If you have an uneasy feeling, he'll say, "But what are you worried about? One way or another it all gets resolved, so what's the big deal?"

JILL: Women are much more willing to share, to talk about clairvoyance, déjà vu, intuition...

EMILY: Gay men do. Do you think it's environmental or genetic?

DORIS: Let me tell you about a conversation I had with two of my friends the other day. Each of us was talking about her health. I was complaining of a sore foot. Flo was giving a lecture on our need for calcium and the dangers of osteoporosis, and Alice was saying her back had kicked out again. Suddenly I rebelled. "Do you hear us?" I cried. "All we talk about now is our medical problems. What happened to the good old days when we talked about sex—you know, who was having an affair with whom?" "You're right," they said, "let's talk about sex." *Ten minutes later we were talking about sex and the terminally ill!*

IRENE: With our friends, I find myself saying, "OK, now the clinic is over." And then the talk turns to restaurants!

NORMA: Isn't that the truth.

IRENE: I know my energies are less, but I have my own program. I walk for forty minutes every morning. I feel better when I do. It's time for myself. I bought a tricycle but I don't ride it.

DORIS: In our household, my husband has headaches. We don't discuss health. At the moment, there's no chronic problem. In a crisis, he's supportive.

NORMA: It's part of a bigger problem, living with someone else's infirmities. My husband hates wearing a hearing aid. It's good that he doesn't have to wear it all the time (we're home so much) but it makes it very difficult.

IRENE: One of my friend's husband was getting hard of hearing. He felt there was nothing wrong, but she finally convinced him to go to an eye, ear, nose and throat man. He went through all the tests and everything checked out fine. So the nurse said to him, "Who referred you?" He said, "My wife." She said, "Eighty percent of our referrals are the wives!"

JILL: So it's a matter of not listening, not not hearing.

EMILY: The first thing your husband will say is, "You're mumbling."

IRENE: Can you at this point in your life change some rules?

DORIS: It's very hard.

JILL: I tell you, you *can* change rules. You take the prerogative—you can make a decision and go ahead instead of asking first, "Should I do this?"

DORIS: It's hard to change the rules.

NORMA: At a certain point you must trust your own judgment. It is something that growing up is about. When I first got married my husband gave me an allowance. Whenever I needed something, I bought something. There was money to pay bills. I had some vague idea of what was there. I wouldn't go out and make a tremendous purchase. And when my husband bought securities, at a certain point the lawyer said it's better to have yours and hers in separate names. It will make it easier later on. At a certain point I suddenly had more time and more inclination. I watched what was going on and I had ideas. I wanted to use my ideas. And I'd ask, "Do you think I ought to do this?" For example, we had Bethlehem Steel since 1941, and steel had been going down. It's just something to invest in. I have the philosophy if you wouldn't go out and buy it now, you shouldn't really hold on to it. So I said, "Don't you think we ought to sell Bethlehem Steel?" But at a certain point I stopped asking and I would go ahead. I'd sell it first and then I'd tell him, "I sold the stock" and I'd put the money in something else. I've had some trades that were successful and some not.

IRENE: We have a savings account that belongs to me to do what I want with it. He knows that. When the tax returns came along he would say to me, "Sign it now and I'll tell you about it later." And I'd say, "Tell me about it first and then I'll sign it." There's a little thing about the husband's name and the wife's name, and his name was on the top all the time and my name was on the bottom and I said to him, "Why can't I be first?" They're little things but they're symbols.

What followed was a general discussion about money with everyone talking at once. On to the Palm Springs area in California.

On a brilliantly sunny day in January (the temperature was seventy-two degrees) six women met for lunch to discuss their lives as wives of retirees. All of them live in communities not far from Palm Springs proper. Once again, it took very little provocation on our part to start the discussion. And yes, we did serve chicken salad.

Introducing:

• *Renee.* Renee's husband is a retired businessman. They are originally from Louisiana but now she and her husband live half of the year in Missouri and half of the year in Indian Wells, California.

• *Nora.* Nora's husband is a retired rancher. Nora and her husband lived in northern California before moving to Indian Wells.

• *Carol.* Carol's husband is a retired golf professional. They are from northern California and lived in Hawaii eleven years before retiring to Indian Wells.

• *Fran.* Fran's husband is a retired city administrator. Fran recently retired from a job of twenty years with a major airline. They come from Chicago and have been living in La Quinta, California, for one year.

• *Betty.* Betty's husband is a retired rancher. They have lived in Palm Desert, California, for many years. Originally they were from England.

• *June.* June's husband is a retired architect. She lives six months a year in New York and six months in Indian Wells.

JUNE: We had heard about Palm Springs for many years, so we came and stayed at the La Quinta Hotel. I had never been to California. We thought it was heaven. The first day at the pool we met a couple who said, "We're buying champagne for everyone because we just bought a condominium, and I said to my husband, "Maybe we should look at condos." The second day another couple at the pool bought champagne to celebrate *their* buying a condominium and I said to him, "We'd better hurry or they're going to run out of houses." Within twenty-four hours, without ever having discussed it before, we bought our retirement home.

FRAN: We'd always wanted to live in Palm Springs. We have been visiting here for twenty-one years and we both agreed that this was the place to be. My husband's very happy being retired. He loves to do what he wants to do when he wants to do it. He likes taking life easy. He's run into some health problems and right now we're learning to cope with that. I hope it's all behind us very shortly.

RENEE: How long we've been retired I really don't know. It seems to have been all my life.

BETTY: My husband retired twice. The first time it really didn't work out. It was boring for him. None of his friends retired at that time, so he was offered a job and he took it and he worked for five more years. This time he retired and it worked out quite well. We have just one home; it's quite adequate. He's been retired for seven years now.

NORA: We have lived here for twenty years. My husband had a little difficulty with so much time on his hands. It took him a while to adjust to retirement but now he's active in tennis and watches the Stock Market. We do have a home in La Jolla where we spend much of our time.

BETTY: Well, there really weren't problems when my husband retired; it was just the kitchen—like he will come in while I'm cooking. It seems he's always just a foot or so behind me. Sometimes I feel like we're the Royal Couple—his Prince Philip trailing my Queen Elizabeth around the kitchen. He'll ask, "What's going on?" and then he'll look in the pantry and say, "You know, we really ought to keep a supply of canned meat." In our house the kitchen faucet drips a little bit if you don't shut it off the right way, and he comes in and says, "You know, you leave the faucet dripping." It's really not my own place anymore. It's OK, he helps me a lot, like he will clear the dishes. He will put the butter dish in the refrigerator, but he forgets to put a new butter in the dish when there's only a teeny bit left. These really aren't problems. They're just minor irritations, that's all.

RENEE: Well, thank goodness for TV. I don't like to watch the programs my husband watches, and he doesn't like the programs that I like, so what he did about that was he bought me a TV to watch what I like. Now he has his own little room to watch his TV, and I have my own little sitting room right off his. When we watch a football game or something we both like then I sit with him. But when he's watching the Stock Market I go in and watch my dumb shows.

FRAN: They like to know you're there. I never carry on much conversation. I don't even know what he's talking about half the time. I say, "Why do you want me to sit in this room if you won't talk to me?" He

	says, "I just want to know that you're here."
RENEE:	When my husband is here alone he gets lonely. When I'm not around he walks all around, he doesn't sleep as well. He's lost.
CAROL:	There are times when your husband can drive you crazy. The only thing I find about my husband being retired is he doesn't get out of his pajamas early enough. He wanders around the house all morning when he's not playing golf. You want to get them dressed and out of the house. He doesn't like to make readjustments, he doesn't like change. He likes the wallpaper the way it is, and it's been there for ten years. He says why change it? I'm the one who likes change. I like new places to live. It doesn't bother me at all leaving any place. I like to be busy, I like to keep moving. In fact, I'm in the travel business.
FRAN:	You're my buddy. I used to work for an airline but I haven't had a chance to take a good trip since I've retired. I'm going to Australia, though.
CAROL:	Are you going to leave your husband home?
FRAN:	Hopefully. I've been ready since October. I've got sand in my shoes.
RENEE:	When I go out for the day, and if he's not there, I write a note to tell him where I'm going. He has no objection, in fact he wants me to go out.
BETTY:	I leave a note, too. My husband fixes his own lunch anyway. That was one of the rules.
JUNE:	What do you mean, *rules*?
BETTY:	When he worked I didn't have to fix his

lunch, so it evolved that I didn't have to fix his lunch when he retired.

NORA: I still feel that I should make his lunch. Since he is home all day and he is around a lot, I still feel the obligation to make sure there's something there for his lunch. When I was asked to the luncheon today I knew we would be in La Jolla, but I really wanted to come. I was a little bit anxious about accepting because I thought that he would say, "That's impossible." I thought he would say, "No, Nora, you can't do it, it will be too much of a drive. It's out of the question." But I really wanted to go, and so, with my mind made up, I approached him. I said to him, "I'm going to this luncheon on Thursday," and he said, "Oh, it's too much driving," and I said, "Well, I'm going to be the one doing the driving." And then he said "OK—OK!"

JUNE: Is it a big departure for you?

NORA: Yes, it is. Since my husband is home, I feel that maybe I should stay home, too, and just take care of his needs and all that kind of stuff. I'm beginning to realize I have a right to leave and there are certain decisions I have to make. He used to rely on me to fill his day. He would say what are we going to do today and I would make suggestions. But I always thought it was just temporary, and that it was up to him to find things to do. Slowly he began to start to find things—tennis, and so forth. But it kind of stayed with me a little bit more and this luncheon today was an example of my beginning to think that I should begin to do things on my own.

CAROL: I don't worry about my husband at all. He's a big boy and he can take care of himself. It's just when he's around the house he's underfoot. I just don't like to have to answer to somebody. I realize you have to answer to your husband but I just don't like that feeling. After all these years, I just want to enjoy him.

FRAN: I've worked for twenty years, and I love it here. I play tennis every day if I can help it. I haven't time to read. I have all these books to read. Sometimes I don't get to read the newspaper until eight o'clock at night. I don't have a chance to be bored.

RENEE: My days are sometimes boring. He plays golf and I don't. I look forward to our visits back to Louisiana. I have relatives there, someone I can talk to. And I enjoy it, the fact that I can get in my car and go the whole day to visit all these different places. I don't have to worry about getting home and fixing anything. Here I'm just more or less tied down. There's just so many times I can go to Palm Springs.

JUNE: Sometimes I feel like the mountains are just like a jail.

CAROL: You do think twice before you drive to La Jolla or San Diego.

JUNE: I finally drove to Rancho Santa Fe and to Los Angeles and it was terrific. I'm going to do that more often.

FRAN: Have you been to Rodeo Drive? We had a little trouble finding it but once we got there it was lovely. We had lunch and then we shopped around and then we started for home at 6 p.m. Do you know what time we got here? Eleven o'clock at night! We made one wrong turn and were on our way to Sacramento. We went to a gas station—there were these Indians and they pointed us one way, and then we went to another gas station and they didn't speak any English, and we had more problems. But he kept saying, "We'll get through. Wait till we get to the next gas station." I was exhausted.

CAROL: If I didn't play golf I wouldn't live here.

RENEE: We're here because my husband likes to play golf—he likes to play a lot. I'm only here because he likes to live here.

JUNE: Carol, if you didn't play golf you said you wouldn't live here. Your husband was a golf pro, so if *you didn't* play you would still almost have to live here.

CAROL: Not necessarily. Not if I gave him enough pressure. [Laughter.] That was sort of a flip remark on my part, but it would be very difficult. I can understand Renee's feelings. Unless you get yourself involved with all the society and benefits and volunteer work and that kind of stuff. That can put you in the hole financially because everything is $2,500 a couple or $5,000 a couple or $80 to go out and participate in a lot of these charities.

RENEE: If you wanted to involve yourself here and get to know the people, and you aren't a golfer or a tennis player, you could become a pink lady at the hospital.

CAROL: You could go to church.

FRAN: My husband makes friends so easily. The man next door—he's from Minnesota—not one night goes by that he doesn't call him. He comes over, takes his shoes off and watches TV at our house. He brings us books on health all the time.

CAROL: I went to a health seminar on Saturday afternoon; Dale Alexander and his philosophy on cod liver oil. In the morning, two glasses of water, one half-hour later one tablespoon cod liver oil and one hour later you have your breakfast.

RENEE: Are you taking it now? Has it helped?

CAROL: I've taken it for about six days. I don't know if I can expect much yet. You have to take it for about a month.

NORA: Did you go to that seminar, Betty?

BETTY: No, I didn't. I just read about it.

CAROL: He wrote a wonderful book. Cod liver oil does wonders for your skin and hair.

JUNE: Do you take it internally or externally? It sounds terrible to down—I was thinking maybe you could rub it on.

FRAN: I don't feel old! And I'm over 65. I don't feel that age at all.

JUNE: You don't look it.

FRAN: Well, I just don't feel it. I mean, I worry about my skin getting all wrinkled out here, you know. What with the sun.

JUNE: Are you going to do anything about it? Like get a lift.

FRAN: I don't know. I had a friend who had something done, and it changed her personality. Really, she looked so much better when she had the creases, when she smiled and she had the wrinkles all around her eyes. I just didn't like her as well after she had it done.

JUNE: I know two women who have had face-lifts and they look great. Is it something, I wonder, where your husband helps you make the decision to do it?

CAROL: It's a big financial investment.

JUNE: If I asked my husband, "Should I have a face-lift?" and he said no, I'd be angry. And if he said yes, I'd be angry because he thinks I need a face-lift! Anyway, I'm afraid of elective surgery.

FRAN: I've never been sick. I've had a couple of hangovers where I was really sick, and he really was very, very good to me. He couldn't do enough. He's got cabinets full of medication, you know, and he would say, "Now try this, or try that," and I said, "Just call the doctor and tell him I want to go to the hospital, I'm going to die." That was horrible. It's never happened since then.

RENEE: My husband has never really been sick, so I don't have any experience with that. But when I had my surgery he couldn't do enough for me. He would do things like fry me an egg—it was like rubber, but I ate it. It was a big thing. The toast was burned, but I just slapped a lot of butter on it. It tasted real good because he fixed it.

JUNE: Do you think a woman should have some space of her very own in the house?

CAROL: Yes. It's my closet in my house, and my bathroom—that's where everything can be disordered. My house is always neat, but my closet is horrendous—I *need* it to be a mess.

JUNE: When he comes home he goes through the house. He likes everything to be shipshape; he's fussy. One day he came in and he said, "What's that spot on the rug?" and I said, "We're going to call a chemist and we're going to find out!" [Laughter.] One man I know went into his wife's kitchen and alphabetized everything—paid no attention to what the things were for—like *a*sparagus, *b*aking soda, all in alphabetical order.

BETTY: My husband handles all of our finances. I know what there is; I had suggested we keep a record. It gives him something to do. He spends time at his desk working on his records every day. Do you discuss money with your husband, Nora?

NORA: Oh, we discuss it, but I just don't have that input because I don't really understand.

FRAN: I think since we've been out here, I don't know why because we're on a smaller income, it seems like we're living higher. I don't know how to account for that feeling. And I'm not as cautious about spending money. We're retired. That's what it's all about. It's like what we've been waiting for. If I see clothes, something I like, I go ahead and get them.

JUNE: Does he say anything?

FRAN: No, he just says go ahead and get it. He wants to get some more warm-ups, and he's got like six. He's been losing weight and they're all baggy on him and falling down, and he wanted me to go and pick up some new ones that were on sale. So I went into his closet and counted out one, two, three, four, five. And I said, "What do you need more for?"

JUNE: What would you do if he did that to you?

FRAN: I'd resent it!

CAROL: I'm on an allowance, to a certain extent. I have so much to run the house on. And when it comes to the big things I have a charge card. My husband is really very kind, but he's in a rut most of the time. He's very happy, and if I want to change something he'll say, "What's wrong with the way it is?" He doesn't want things changed. Today I changed the sliding door on the patio. It used to slide on the left side, and now you come in on the right. And I moved the table and all, because I get tired of things in the same place.

	So when he comes home he's going to have to come in on the other side of the patio.
NORA:	What'll he do?
CAROL:	Oh, he'll learn, because one side is locked and the other side is open.
BETTY:	You know, we live in a quite unrealistic part of the world. There has to be a balance, I feel, between work and play. We're playing all the time out here. And if I don't do some work then I can't enjoy my play. I clean my own house and we do our own yard work and it is only then that I can enjoy going out to play tennis and have the other side of the coin. I think you also have to become a little bit more considerate of each other. If I have something to do I say to my husband, "I'm going out, do you want to come, too?
CAROL:	I really should watch my tongue and treat my husband with more kindness. Because he's around all the time and I see him all the time, I get flip in my answers. It's really lovely having him around and I don't mean to be so short when I speak to him. It's a good thing he understands me.
FRAN:	I have to leave now. My husband has a doctor's appointment and I promised I'd get back in time to take him. It was a lovely luncheon and, Carol, if you ever go on a trip and need someone to go with you, call me. I'm half packed all the time.

And so two successful luncheons came to an end. Given the fact that the women were not intimate friends, it was interesting to see how willing they were to share personal observations and feelings with each other. There were laughs at both the luncheons. We don't presume to suggest that these two meetings ex-

posed any profound difficulties the women might be
facing at this particular stage of life, but still there are
some interesting deductions to be made:

- The women in both groups, whether they realized
  it or not, were dealing with the very timely subject
  of equality and independence, just as women of the
  younger generation are.
- The women in Chicago seemed to be more conscious of personal identity. The women in California were more concerned with health, fitness and
  appearance.
- Both groups of women had a sense of "territorial
  invasion" when their husbands retired.
- The women in both groups were somewhat balky
  at having to be their husbands' nurturers at this
  time of life.
- Despite carping at minor irritations, all of them
  expressed commitment to their marriages and affection for their husbands.
- They all had a sense of humor, and felt they were
  lucky to be able to enjoy the rewards of retirement
  life.

No doubt you've reached your own conclusions after
meeting these women at lunch.

10
HAPPILY EVER AFTER

You've met many women in this book who are living out the retirement years with their husbands just as you are. Some you've probably liked, some you've probably disagreed with and many you've probably not only recognized but identified with.

Despite petty gripes, occasional differences and rough periods of adjustment, these women are in marriages that work. Some better than others, it's true, but of the seventy-five women interviewed there was only one who confessed that her marriage was in serious trouble, and she and her husband were seeking professional advice. After the number of years these couples have invested in their marriages it would be rare for them to think of divorce as a solution.

The retirement years are supposed to be the golden years, the years of fulfilled promises. And they were for most of the couples in this book. However, there were some husbands who after years of work did not experience the expected payoff. For them retirement was painful. They mourned their loss of identity and felt insecure with the sudden lack of structure in their lives. Their wives, for the most part, were sensitive to their reactions, but the responses varied. A number of women tried to orchestrate their husbands' retirement lives, feeling that "if he can just keep busy he'll be all right." These same women were hurt and angry when their suggestions were rebuffed. Other wives resented having to be nurturers at this time of life. But most of them felt their husband's anguish and tried a variety of ways to help them get through it.

Many of the women experienced guilt and anger because they couldn't solve their husbands' problems. There was a tendency to blame their husbands for making demands, when in reality it wasn't their husbands' demands which frustrated them but the demands they made on themselves. So many of the wives assumed the full responsibility for their husbands' lack of immediate adjustment to retirement. They felt that they should have the magic ability to do for their husbands what they had always done for their children—"make it all better." What is curious about their reactions is that they had much more patience with their own mood swings. They had weathered the stresses of child rearing, separation from children, and menopause, and had insight into their feelings. But being unable to help their husbands, men they loved and looked to for emotional security, adjust to their newfound leisure was often frustrating.

There were, of course, some women who had an uncanny ability to make the transition to retirement life smoothly. What struck us about these women was their patience and their optimism. They knew that they were going through a rough patch but were convinced it was only temporary and were confident that all would work out. They were supportive of their husbands without hovering. They struck a healthy balance by spending time with their husbands and continuing to live their own lives as well. Most important, they were not burdened by the baggage of guilt. Their relationships with their husbands can be characterized as adult-to-adult rather than mother-to-child.

THEIR OWN FEARS

The women not only had their husbands' anxieties to deal with; many expressed their personal fears. They were worried about money. Some pictured themselves having to scrimp and save for the rest of their lives and many admitted they had only a hazy idea of their financial situations. The majority of the women interviewed took little or no part in the handling of family finances. Those who did take an active part in money management expressed no fear about money.

More than their fears about finances were their fears that their husbands would move in on their territory. Would they be underfoot in the kitchen? Would they want to take over the whole house? To our surprise not as many women as we would have thought were delighted at the prospect of their husbands' taking over some of the household duties. They saw their territory invaded and their control being usurped. It is our conclusion that a woman's desire to protect her territory from her husband's control is a sign of a deeper concern with their sudden reversal of roles. For the years of her marriage to him she has seen her husband as aggressive, the breadwinner, involved in what she considered "masculine" pursuits. With retirement he seems to have taken on a passive role, has become interested in her world and starts doing what she considers to be feminine things. The irony of the situation is that his new attitude appears at the very time when she is ready to retire from the role as nest maker. Yet she doesn't always recognize his retirement as an opportunity to expand her own horizons.

Despite the initial feelings of unease when this role reversal took place, the women adjusted within the first few years of retirement and became comfortable with it.

TIME HELPS

Since our study has taken us over a year, it has given us an opportunity to meet with a number of the women more than once. In the first few months we met with several women who were making the initial transition to retirement life and were finding it extremely painful. They complained of feelings of suffocation because of the constant presence of their husbands. One year later all of the situations had improved. Resentments had diminished, and many of their problems had been solved.

As one woman put it, "I started to do what's best for me. I was so busy trying to solve his problems I forgot about my needs. Things are so much better now. It just took us some time to work things out."

There were several women who were still chafing at the restraints of their husbands' retirements one year later, and there is one woman we interviewed who has been in a low-level conflict with her husband for five years. It seems that these women choose to keep it this way.

Most of the gripes were petty ones: "He wants to stay in his pajamas all morning." "He does nothing but watch television." "He monitors all of my phone calls." Almost all of these annoyances were related with a laugh, which brings us to the following imperative: YOU MUST KEEP YOUR SENSE OF HUMOR!

Hopefully, many of the stories in this book did make you smile. When you read about someone else's husband complaining about her buying seven cans of anchovies, didn't you find it amusing? If *your* husband had said it, would you have seen the humor? If not at the moment it happened, certainly you should have laughed later on. As long as the two of you laugh together, as long as you can both stop and see the humor of a situation that a minute before was unnecessarily grim, you are not in trouble. Try to use your humor to ease tense situations. You've heard the old cliché, don't laugh at him, laugh with him. Well, it won't even hurt to laugh at him once in a while. And above all, laugh at yourself.

PREPARE FOR THE FUTURE

We were most impressed by the women we interviewed. They were concerned about their husbands, and many were exceptionally creative in helping their spouses through this period of adjustment. They were active and vital enough to know that change was still possible. None of them looked upon the retirement years as an end; they considered these years a beginning and felt that the future held exciting possibilities.

Marriage and family counselor Nancy Ackerman suggests that couples facing retirement sit down and talk about their expectations of each other. She goes so far as to suggest that couples would do well to write out the rules of retirement, or to make a contract with each other so that neither is surprised by the other's expectations. Not a bad idea.

If writing a contract seems too formal to you and if communication is sometimes difficult, in the next chapter we offer you and your husband a set of work sheets. These should serve as guides for productive discussions and should help you anticipate the problems you and your husband might face in retirement. We hope that working on these discussion questions together will solve your problems before they arise. We also hope that the two of you will learn things about each other you never knew despite your many years of successful marriage.

11
WORKBOOK
FOR
RETIREMENT

Now is the time to take stock of the potential you and your husband have for a successful retirement. The work sheets that follow should help to dissipate the difficulties you both have in communicating your needs and negotiating your expectations. Work on these pages together and be sure to follow these instructions:

Instructions

1. Answer the questions on those pages designated *Her Questions*.
2. Have your husband answer the questions on those pages designated *His Questions*.
3. Both of you must be honest in your answers. Understand that all these points are to be negotiated.
4. When you have each completed a section, such as the questions on *Doing Things Separately*, get together and compare your answers.
5. Don't argue.
6. Go through the questions and pick out all of

those on which you agree. Congratulate yourselves. No need to worry about comunication
here.

7. Now focus on those questions on which you disagree.
8. Don't argue.
9. It's time to do some communicating, some negotiating. For example: If you have answered
   no to the question *Do you feel it is your responsibility to find activities for him to fill his
   time now that he has retired?* and he has answered *yes* to the question *Do you expect your
   wife to help you find activities to fill your day?*,
   it's time for the two of you to do some talking.

What could follow is a dialogue that goes something
like this:

YOU: It's that word *responsibility* in the question
that worries me. I don't think anyone can
be responsible for anyone else's time.

HE: I don't expect you to be responsible, but I
would like it if you took an interest in things
I like to do or made suggestions for things
we could do together.

YOU: Oh, I'd like doing that. But sometimes I'm
afraid to suggest things because you don't
always like what I suggest.

HE: I don't mind your making suggestions. As
long as you don't mind my not taking you
up on every one of them.

YOU: OK. I'll keep an eye out for things that
might interest you, and I'll take an interest
in what you do as long as you don't make
me feel responsible for your time.

HE: I agree. You're not responsible for my time.
In fact, I'm thinking of taking a basic computer course at the junior college.

YOU: I think that's terrific.

HE: Do you want to take it with me?

We're not saying that this is the way it would happen, word for word, in your family. But we are saying that things are better discussed than being left unsaid. In the following pages there are enough questions to keep the two of you communicating for the next six months.

DOING THINGS SEPARATELY
Her Questions

1. Do you expect to spend your daytime hours with your husband?

      ____ Yes ____ No

2. Do you expect to continue your present daytime routine, even though your activities do not include him?

      ____ Yes ____ No

3. Do you expect to make some changes in your daytime routine, for example, keeping your volunteer job but giving up your weekly bridge game, now that he is retired?

      ____ Yes ____ No

4. Do you expect him to fill his own time during the day now that he is retired?

      ____ Yes ____ No

5. Do you feel it is your responsibility to find activities for him to fill his time now that he is retired?

      ____ Yes ____ No

6. Do you think you should ask your husband if it is all right for you to go out to spend an afternoon with your friends?

      ____ Yes ____ No

7. Do you think you should tell your husband your plans the day before you go out?

      ____ Yes ____ No

8. Would you entertain your women friends in your home while your husband is home?

_____ Yes _____ No

9. If you do entertain your friends, would you ask him to join you and to visit for a while?

_____ Yes _____ No

10. Do you expect to see less of your women friends now that your husband is retired?

_____ Yes _____ No

11. Do you see the kitchen as your territory?

_____ Yes _____ No

12. Do you dread his taking over as chef in your kitchen?

_____ Yes _____ No

13. Do you expect him to share the household tasks now that he is retired?

_____ Yes _____ No

14. Would you want him to do some of the grocery shopping?

_____ Yes _____ No

When your husband completes his quiz, compare his answers with yours. Talk over those answers on which you disagree.

DOING THINGS SEPARATELY
His Questions

1. Do you expect your wife to spend her daytime hours with you now that you are retired?

    ＿＿ Yes ＿＿ No

2. Do you expect her to continue to do the things she always did in the daytime and not change her routine now that you are home?

    ＿＿ Yes ＿＿ No

3. Do you expect her to make some changes in her daytime routine, for example, should she give up her weekly bridge game but keep her volunteer job?

    ＿＿ Yes ＿＿ No

4. Do you feel you can fill your own free time during the day now that you are retired?

    ＿＿ Yes ＿＿ No

5. Do you expect your wife to help you find activities to fulfill your day?

    ＿＿ Yes ＿＿ No

6. Should your wife ask you if it's all right if she goes out?

    ＿＿ Yes ＿＿ No

7. Should your wife tell you if she has plans to go out on the next day?

    ＿＿ Yes ＿＿ No

8. Would you mind her entertaining her women friends at home while you are there?

    ＿＿ Yes ＿＿ No

9. If she does entertain her friends while you are at home, would you like to join them for a while?

_____ Yes _____ No

10. Do you expect your wife to see less of her women friends now that you are retired?

_____ Yes _____ No

11. Do you see the kitchen as you wife's territory?

_____ Yes _____ No

12. Would you like to cook some special recipes in the kitchen on occasion?

_____ Yes _____ No

13. Would you be willing to share the household tasks now that you are retired?

_____ Yes _____ No

14. Would you be willing to do some of the grocery shopping?

_____ Yes _____ No

When your wife completes her quiz, compare your answers with hers and start your discussion.

DOING THINGS TOGETHER
Her Questions

1. Do you have a hobby?

   ＿＿ Yes ＿＿ No

2. Does your husband participate with you in that hobby?

   ＿＿ Yes ＿＿ No

3. Would you like him to?

   ＿＿ Yes ＿＿ No

4. Check any of the following activities that you enjoy:

   ＿＿ theater ＿＿ ballet ＿＿ concerts
   ＿＿ museums ＿＿ movies ＿＿ football
   ＿＿ basketball ＿＿ baseball ＿＿ other

5. Check the activities in which you enjoy participating:

   ＿＿ playing tennis ＿＿ fishing
   ＿＿ playing golf ＿＿ swimming
   ＿＿ square dancing ＿＿ other

6. Are you interested in taking courses?

   ＿＿ Yes ＿＿ No

7. Do you enjoy watching television?

   ＿＿ Yes ＿＿ No

8. Do you enjoy driving?

   ＿＿ Yes ＿＿ No

9. Would you enjoy taking two- and three-day trips?

   ＿＿ Yes ＿＿ No

10. Would you cheerfully attend an event in which you are not very interested simply because your husband wants to attend?

_____ Yes _____ No

11. Would you attend an event that your husband enjoys if he, in turn, was willing to attend an event that you enjoy?

_____ Yes _____ No

12. Do you enjoy walking?

_____ Yes _____ No

13. Do you enjoy dining out?

_____ Yes _____ No

14. Do you enjoy shopping?

_____ Yes _____ No

15. Do you like playing games?

_____ Yes _____ No

(Check the games you enjoy.)
_____ cards   _____ Trivial   _____ Scrabble
_____ Monopoly   Pursuit   _____ other

16. Do you enjoy making love in the afternoon?

_____ Yes _____ No

If you agree on five or more things you mutually enjoy and are willing to do together you are like most successfully married couples and have a good thing going.

If you agree on ten or more things you mutually enjoy and are willing to do together, yours is an amazing relationship. Remember, it isn't necessary to do *everything* together.

DOING THINGS TOGETHER
His Questions

1. Do you have a hobby?

   ＿＿＿ Yes ＿＿＿ No

2. Does your wife participate with you in that hobby?

   ＿＿＿ Yes ＿＿＿ No

3. Would you like her to?

   ＿＿＿ Yes ＿＿＿ No

4. Check any of the following activities that you enjoy:

   ＿＿＿ theater ＿＿＿ ballet ＿＿＿ concerts
   ＿＿＿ museums ＿＿＿ movies ＿＿＿ football
   ＿＿＿ basketball ＿＿＿ baseball ＿＿＿ other

5. Check the activities in which you enjoy participating:

   ＿＿＿ playing tennis ＿＿＿ fishing
   ＿＿＿ playing golf ＿＿＿ swimming
   ＿＿＿ square dancing ＿＿＿ other

6. Are you interested in taking courses?

   ＿＿＿ Yes ＿＿＿ No

7. Do you enjoy watching television?

   ＿＿＿ Yes ＿＿＿ No

8. Do you enjoy driving?

   ＿＿＿ Yes ＿＿＿ No

9. Would you enjoy taking two- and three-day trips?

   ＿＿＿ Yes ＿＿＿ No

10. Would you cheerfully attend an event in which you are not very interested simply because your wife wants to attend?

_____ Yes _____ No

11. Would you attend an event that your wife enjoys if she, in turn, was willing to attend an event that you enjoy?

_____ Yes _____ No

12. Do you enjoy walking?

_____ Yes _____ No

13. Do you enjoy dining out?

_____ Yes _____ No

14. Do you enjoy shopping?

_____ Yes _____ No

15. Do you like playing games?

_____ Yes _____ No

(Check the games you enjoy)
_____ cards   _____ Trivial   _____ Scrabble
_____ Monopoly   Pursuit   _____ other

16. Do you enjoy making love in the afternoon?

_____ Yes _____ No

HITTING THE ROAD
Her Questions

1. Do you enjoy travel?

   _____ Yes _____ No

2. Do you wish your husband would be willing to travel more?

   _____ Yes _____ No

3. Check the places in the world you would like to visit:
   _____ Continental   _____ Canada   _____ Mexico
   U.S.   _____ Europe   _____ Asia
   _____ South   _____ Australia _____ Others
   America   _____ Africa

5. Do you prefer guided tours?

   _____ Yes _____ No

5. Do you prefer to make your own travel arrangements?

   _____ Yes _____ No

6. Do you object to any of these modes of travel?
   _____ flying   _____ long drives _____ train rides
   _____ bus rides   _____ other

7. Do you mind economizing on transportation and living arrangements when you travel?

   _____ Yes _____ No

8. Do you mind roughing it when you travel (sharing bathroom facilities, staying in hostels, etc.)?

   _____ Yes _____ No

9. Do you like to go camping?

_____ Yes _____ No

10. Do you have a trip in mind now that you really want to take?

_____ Yes _____ No

11. Have you discussed it with your husband?

_____ Yes _____ No

12. Do you occasionally like to take a trip without your husband?

_____ Yes _____ No

13. Would you mind if your husband took a trip without you?

_____ Yes _____ No

HITTING THE ROAD
His Questions

1. Do you enjoy travel?

    ____ Yes ____ No

2. Do you wish your wife would be willing to travel more?

    ____ Yes ____ No

3. Check the places in the world you would like to visit:

    ____ Continental   ____ Canada   ____ Mexico
         U.S.   ____ Europe   ____ Asia
    ____ South   ____ Australia ____ Others
         America   ____ Africa

4. Do you prefer guided tours?

    ____ Yes ____ No

5. Do you prefer to make your own travel arrangements?

    ____ Yes ____ No

6. Do you object to any of these modes of travel?

    ____ flying   ____ long drives ____ train rides
    ____ bus rides   ____ other

7. Do you mind economizing on transportation and living arrangements when you travel?

    ____ Yes ____ No

8. Do you mind roughing it when you travel (sharing bathroom facilities, staying in hostels, etc.)?

    ____ Yes ____ No

9. Do you like to go camping?

_____ Yes _____ No

10. Do you have a trip in mind now that you really want to take?

_____ Yes _____ No

11. Have you discussed it with your wife?

_____ Yes _____ No

12. Do you occasionally like to take a trip without your wife?

_____ Yes _____ No

13. Would you mind if your wife took a trip without you?

_____ Yes _____ No

SHE WORKS, HE DOESN'T
Her Questions

Note: If the job market does not interest you, skip this questionnaire and go on to the next one.

1. Do you have a job now?

   _____ Yes _____ No

2. Would you like to get a job now that your husband is retired?

   _____ Yes _____ No

3. Would you like to quit your job now that your husband is retired?

   _____ Yes _____ No

4. Do you work for any of the following reasons?
   _____ intellectual stimulation and social contacts
   _____ money   _____ health   _____ self-esteem
                        benefits
   _____ to get away from the house

5. Do you feel trapped in your job?

   _____ Yes _____ No

6. Is your husband willing to take on some of the domestic duties now that you are working and he is not?

   _____ Yes _____ No

7. What domestic duties would you particularly like him to assume? _____

8. Is the money you earn *your* money to be spent as you see fit?

   _____ Yes _____ No

9. Do you think that the money you earn should go into your joint account?

_____ Yes _____ No

10. If you do work are you involved in office social activities?

_____ Yes _____ No

11. Is it possible for your husband to join in these activities?

_____ Yes _____ No

12. Do you think the outside contacts you've made in the marketplace make your relationship with your husband at home more interesting?

_____ Yes _____ No

13. Are you planning to get a job, now that your husband is retired?

_____ Yes _____ No

14. Would your husband object to your working at home?

_____ Yes _____ No

15. Would he be willing to give you the privacy you need to work at home?

_____ Yes _____ No

SHE WORKS, HE DOESN'T
His Questions

1. Does your wife have a job now?

   _____ Yes _____ No

2. Would you object to her getting a job if she is not working now?

   _____ Yes _____ No

3. Would you like her to quit her job now that you are retired?

   _____ Yes _____ No

4. For which of the following reasons do you believe she works:

   _____ intellectual stimulation and social contacts

   _____ money   _____ health   _____ self-esteem
   benefits

   _____ to get away from the house

5. Do you think she is content in her job?

   _____ Yes _____ No

6. Are you willing to take on some of the domestic duties now that she is working and you are not?

   _____ Yes _____ No

7. Which domestic duties would you be willing to assume? _____

8. Is the money your wife earns to be spent as *she* sees fit?

   _____ Yes _____ No

9. Do you think that the money your wife earns should go into your joint account?

_____ Yes _____ No

10. If she does work, do you mind the time she spends involved in her office social activities?

_____ Yes _____ No

11. Is it possible for you to join in these activities?

_____ Yes _____ No

12. If so, would you want to?

_____ Yes _____ No

13. Do you think the outside contacts she has made in the marketplace have made your relationship with her at home more interesting?

_____ Yes _____ No

14. Would you object to her working at home?

_____ Yes _____ No

15. If she worked at home, would you be willing to give her the privacy she needs?

_____ Yes _____ No

FRICTION OVER FINANCES
Her Questions

1. Do you have a good grasp of your present financial situation?

   ____ Yes ____ No

2. Do you want to know more about your finances?

   ____ Yes ____ No

3. Do you worry about having enough money to live comfortably in retirement?

   ____ Yes ____ No

4. If you do worry, are these concerns based on the reality of your financial worth?

   ____ Yes ____ No

5. Does your husband hold the purse strings?

   ____ Yes ____ No

6. Do you prefer it that way?

   ____ Yes ____ No

7. Do you hold the purse strings?

   ____ Yes ____ No

8. Do you prefer it that way?

   ____ Yes ____ No

9. Do you decide on major purchases and investments together?

   ____ Yes ____ No

10. Do you feel you are inclined to be extravagant about money?

    ____ Yes ____ No

11. Do you feel he is extravagant about money?

    ____ Yes ____ No

12. Do you have a will?

    ____ Yes ____ No

13. Have you discussed the matters of his estate, his insurance and his will with your husband?

    ____ Yes ____ No

14. Do you think it's a touchy subject?

    ____ Yes ____ No

15. Do you have a book with a complete account of your financial records?

    ____ Yes ____ No

16. Do you have a safe-deposit box and do you know where the key is?

    ____ Yes ____ No

17. Are you willing to be more conservative in your spending now that your husband is retired?

    ____ Yes ____ No

18. Do you admit to any quirky economies— undertipping, looking for parking meters that haven't expired—that might make friends think you're cheap?

    ____ Yes ____ No

19. Does your husband have quirky economies?

    ____ Yes ____ No

20. Does it bother you?

    ____ Yes ____ No

We realize that money is a loaded subject, and the questions are not intended to cause friction between you and your spouse. Instead, your honesty with each other should remove the charge from the subject. For example, if you've been uncomfortable talking about his will or his insurance with him, the questionnaire should help initiate the subject for you.

FRICTION OVER FINANCES
His Questions

1. Does your wife have a good grasp of your present financial situation?

    ____ Yes ____ No

2. Do you want her to know more about your finances?

    ____ Yes ____ No

3. Do you worry about having enough money to live comfortably in retirement?

    ____ Yes ____ No

4. If you do worry, are these concerns based on the reality of your financial worth?

    ____ Yes ____ No

5. Do you hold the purse strings?

    ____ Yes ____ No

6. Do you prefer it that way?

    ____ Yes ____ No

7. Does your wife hold the purse strings?

    ____ Yes ____ No

8. Do you prefer it that way?

    ____ Yes ____ No

9. Do you decide on major purchases and investments together?

    ____ Yes ____ No

10. Do you feel your wife is extravagant about money?

    ____ Yes ____ No

11. Do you feel you are inclined to be extravagant about money?

_____ Yes _____ No

12. Do you have a will?

_____ Yes _____ No

13. Have you discussed the matters of your estate, your insurance and your will with your wife?

_____ Yes _____ No

14. Do you think it's a touchy subject?

_____ Yes _____ No

15. Do you have a book with a complete account of your financial records?

_____ Yes _____ No

16. Do you have a safe-deposit box and do you know where the key is?

_____ Yes _____ No

17. Are you more conservative in your spending now that you are retired?

_____ Yes _____ No

18. Do you admit to any quirky economies— undertipping, looking for parking meters that haven't expired—that might make friends think you're cheap?

_____ Yes _____ No

19. Does your wife have any quirky economies?

_____ Yes _____ No

20. Does it bother you?

_____ Yes _____ No

MAKING THE BIG MOVE
Her Questions

If you are both content living where you are now, go on to the next work sheet. If not, answer the questions below. If you are content but he is not, ask him to answer his questionnaire and go over the answers together.

1. Do you wish to move from your present residence?

   _____ Yes _____ No

2. Do you think you should move because of any of the following reasons:
   _____ economics _____ weather _____ health
   _____ change of scene _____ other

3. Do you want to move to a smaller residence?

   _____ Yes _____ No

4. Do you want to move to:
   _____ a house _____ an apartment
   _____ a condominium _____ other

5. Do you want to move to:
   _____ the city _____ the suburbs _____ the country

6. Do you want to move to another part of the country?

   _____ Yes _____ No

7. Which part of the country:
   _____ Midwest _____ West _____ Northwest
   _____ South _____ Northeast _____ out of the country

8. Would you want to live in a retirement village?

_____ Yes _____ No

9. Do you make friends easily?

_____ Yes _____ No

10. Do you worry about making friends in a new community?

_____ Yes _____ No

11. Do you have a community in mind to move to where you already have friends?

_____ Yes _____ No

12. Would moving take you away from important members of your family?

_____ Yes _____ No

13. Would you miss these members of your family?

_____ Yes _____ No

14. Would you pass up moving rather than leave members of your family?

_____ Yes _____ No

MAKING THE BIG MOVE
His Questions

1. Do you wish to move from your present residence?

   _____ Yes _____ No

2. Do you think you should move because of any of the following reasons:

   _____ economics _____ weather _____ health
   _____ change of scene _____ other

3. Do you want to move to a smaller residence?

   _____ Yes _____ No

4. Do you want to move to:

   _____ a house   _____ an apartment
   _____ a condominium   _____ other

5. Do you want to move to:

   _____ the city   _____ the   _____ the
                     suburbs   country

6. Do you want to move to another part of the country?

   _____ Yes _____ No

7. Which part of the country?

   _____ Midwest   _____ West   _____ Northwest
   _____ South   _____ Northeast _____ out of the
                                         country

8. Would you want to live in a retirement village?

   _____ Yes _____ No

9. Do you make friends easily?

   _____ Yes _____ No

10. Do you worry about making friends in a new community?

　　　　　　　　＿＿ Yes ＿＿ No

11. Do you have a community in mind to move to where you already have friends?

　　　　　　　　＿＿ Yes ＿＿ No

12. Would moving take you away from important members of your family?

　　　　　　　　＿＿ Yes ＿＿ No

13. Would you miss these members of your family?

　　　　　　　　＿＿ Yes ＿＿ No

14. Would you pass up moving rather than leave members of your family?

　　　　　　　　＿＿ Yes ＿＿ No

STAYING HEALTHY
Her Questions

Diet and Exercise

1. Do you or your husband have to diet?

   _____ Yes _____ No

2. Do you try to cooperate and help your husband in his diet?

   _____ Yes _____ No

3. Do you nag or criticize your husband when he goes off his diet?

   _____ Yes _____ No

4. If you do, have you found it productive?

   _____ Yes _____ No

5. Does your husband nag or criticize you?

   _____ Yes _____ No

6. Does it help you?

   _____ Yes _____ No

   Defeat you?

   _____ Yes _____ No

7. Would you like to go to a health spa?

   _____ Yes _____ No

8. Do you take brisk walks on a regular basis?

   _____ Yes _____ No

9. Would you be more inclined to walk on a regular basis if your husband walked with you?

   _____ Yes _____ No

10. Do you engage in sports activities such as golf, tennis, swimming, jogging or bicycling?

_____ Yes _____ No

11. Would you engage in sports more regularly if your husband joined you?

_____ Yes _____ No

12. Are you considering plastic surgery?

_____ Yes _____ No

13. Does your husband know you are considering it? How do you think he feels about it? _____

Alcohol

1. Do you drink to "calm your nerves?"

_____ Yes _____ No

2. Do you drink to get comfortable in social situations?

_____ Yes _____ No

3. Have you noticed you have less tolerance for alcohol than you used to?

_____ Yes _____ No

4. Do you feel guilty about your drinking?

_____ Yes _____ No

5. Now that your husband is home during the day, does your cocktail hour start earlier and last longer?

_____ Yes _____ No

6. Do you have drinks daily?

_____ Yes _____ No

7. Do you drink when you're alone?

_____ Yes _____ No

8. Do you wish your husband would drink less?

_____ Yes _____ No

Drugs

1. Do you take prescription medicine from more than one doctor?

_____ Yes _____ No

2. Do you keep your physicians informed as to *all* the medication you are taking?

_____ Yes _____ No

3. Do you ever give your medicine to your husband or friends?

_____ Yes _____ No

4. Do you ever take medicine given to you by well-meaning friends?

_____ Yes _____ No

Yourselves

1. Are you content with your sexual relationship?

_____ Yes _____ No

2. Are you willing to talk openly with your husband about your sexual relationship?

_____ Yes _____ No

STAYING HEALTHY
His Questions

Diet and Exercise

1. Do you or your wife have to diet?

    _____ Yes _____ No

2. Do you try to cooperate and help your wife in her diet?

    _____ Yes _____ No

3. Do you nag or criticize your wife when she goes off her diet?

    _____ Yes _____ No

4. If you do, have you found it productive?

    _____ Yes _____ No

5. Does your wife nag or criticize you?

    _____ Yes _____ No

6. Does it help you?

    _____ Yes _____ No

    Defeat you?

    _____ Yes _____ No

7. Would you like to go to a health spa?

    _____ Yes _____ No

8. Do you take brisk walks on a regular basis?

    _____ Yes _____ No

9. Would you be more inclined to walk on a regular basis if your wife walked with you?

    _____ Yes _____ No

10. Do you engage in sports activities such as golf, tennis, swimming, jogging or bicycling?

_____ Yes _____ No

11. Would you engage in sports more regularly if your wife joined you?

_____ Yes _____ No

12. Do you believe your wife is considering plastic surgery?

_____ Yes _____ No

13. If so, how do you feel about it? _____

Alcohol

1. Do you drink alcohol on a regular basis each day?

_____ Yes _____ No

2. Does your wife drink to get comfortable in social situations?

_____ Yes _____ No

3. Have you noticed you have less tolerance for alcohol than you used to?

_____ Yes _____ No

4. Do you feel guilty about your drinking?

_____ Yes _____ No

5. Now that you are home during the day, does your cocktail hour start earlier and last longer?

_____ Yes _____ No

6. Does your wife have drinks daily?

_____ Yes _____ No

7. Do you drink when you're alone?

_____ Yes _____ No

8. Do you wish your wife would drink less?

_____ Yes _____ No

Drugs

1. Do you take prescription medicine from more than one doctor?

_____ Yes _____ No

2. Do you keep your physicians informed as to *all* the medication you are taking?

_____ Yes _____ No

3. Do you ever give your medicine to your wife or friends?

_____ Yes _____ No

4. Do you ever take medicine originally prescribed for your wife?

_____ Yes _____ No

Yourselves

1. Are you content with your sexual relationship?

_____ Yes _____ No

2. Are you willing to talk openly with your wife about your sexual relationship?

_____ Yes _____ No

PLAN YOUR DAY
Her Questions

1. What time do you usually get up? _____

2. What time does your husband get up? _____

3. Would you like him to get up earlier? _____
   later? _____ doesn't matter _____

4. Do you eat breakfast together?
   _____ Yes _____ No

5. Would you like to have breakfast together?
   _____ Yes _____ No

6. Do the two of you plan your day's activities in
   the morning?
   _____ Yes _____ No

7. Do you share household chores?
   _____ Yes _____ No

8. What household tasks would you like him to
   take over:
   _____ shopping   _____ cooking
   _____ laundry   _____ cleaning

9. Do you plan the day's meals together?
   _____ Yes _____ No

10. Do you go your separate ways most days?
    _____ Yes _____ No

11. Do you prefer it that way?
    _____ Yes _____ No

12. Do the two of you participate in activities together every day?

      _____ Yes _____ No

13. Do you prefer it that way?

      _____ Yes _____ No

14. Do you rendezvous with your husband for tea or cocktails in the late afternoon to share confidences?

      _____ Yes _____ No

15. Would you like to?

      _____ Yes _____ No

16. Do you have a satisfactory social life?

      _____ Yes _____ No

17. Would you like to socialize more than you do?

      _____ Yes _____ No

18. Do you both go to bed at the same time?

      _____ Yes _____ No

19. Have you reached a satisfactory sexual accommodation with each other?

      _____ Yes _____ No

Compare your answers. You should have a lot to talk about. Happy retirement!

PLAN YOUR DAY
His Questions

1. What time do you usually get up? _____

2. What time does your wife get up? _____

3. Would you like her to get up earlier? _____
   later? _____ doesn't matter _____

4. Do you eat breakfast together?
   _____ Yes _____ No

5. Would you like to have breakfast together?
   _____ Yes _____ No

6. Do the two of you plan your day's activities in the morning?
   _____ Yes _____ No

7. Do you share household chores?
   _____ Yes _____ No

8. What household tasks would you be willing to take over:
   _____ shopping   _____ cooking
   _____ laundry   _____ cleaning

9. Do you plan the day's meals together?
   _____ Yes _____ No

10. Do you go your separate ways most days?
    _____ Yes _____ No

11. Do you prefer it that way?
    _____ Yes _____ No

12. Do the two of you participate in activities together every day?

_____ Yes _____ No

13. Do you prefer it that way?

_____ Yes _____ No

14. Do you rendezvous with your wife for tea or cocktails in the late afternoon to share confidences?

_____ Yes _____ No

15. Would you like to?

_____ Yes _____ No

16. Do you have a satisfactory social life?

_____ Yes _____ No

17. Would you like to socialize more than you do?

_____ Yes _____ No

18. Do you both go to bed at the same time?

_____ Yes _____ No

19. Have you reached a satisfactory sexual accommodation with each other?

_____ Yes _____ No